Democracy, Fascism and the
New World Order

Those who invest all their energies and hopes in an undertaking even tinged with depravity are bound to its success and are apt to acquire an obscure self-contempt which qualifies their faith, first in their fellows, and then in themselves.

Michael Oakeshott, 'The Tower of Babel'

Democracy, Fascism and the New World Order

Ivo Mosley

ia

IMPRINT ACADEMIC

Published in the UK by Imprint Academic
PO Box 200, Exeter EX5 5YX, UK

Published in the USA by Imprint Academic
Philosophy Documentation Center
PO Box 7147, Charlottesville, VA 22906-7147, USA

ISBN 0 907845 649

A CIP catalogue record for this book is available from the
British Library and US Library of Congress

Contents

Acknowledgements

I can't acknowledge by name all the people whose conversations have informed this book. Some might lose their jobs and others I've forgotten. But I hereby thank them all nonetheless.

Most thanks of all are due to Keith Sutherland, who encouraged this project and is prepared to publish it now it's complete. He demanded high standards from my lazy brain, and I hope he got them.

And finally I'd like to thank in advance anyone who buys this book. I need the money.

Introduction

*Now power is of its nature evil, whoever wields it. It is not stability but a
lust and therefore insatiable, unhappy in itself and doomed to make others
unhappy.*   Jacob Burckhardt

*If you gain every morsel of your bread from the powers that be, and you
wish to be sure of getting that little bit extra, then you are wise to give up
thinking altogether*   Nadezhda Mandelstam.

'Democracy is the worst form of government in the world —
except for all the rest!' With these words, Winston Churchill
expressed a quandary of the modern age: that whatever the
disappointments of democracy, other forms of government
throw up horrors even worse. Not only that; other methods of
government are inconceivable to us, because as free people we
naturally expect a role in choosing who governs us.

Yet there is a widening gap between what we expect of
democracy and what it has actually turned out to be. When
'democracy' is limited to throwing out one bunch of rogues
every few years only to let another bunch in; when it demands
more and more regulation and scrutiny of our lives while
delivering more and more inept and wasteful management;
when it ignores problems which concern us all such as drugs
and environmental degradation but is keen to rush off to war;
when we are suspicious of the truth or falsehood of the every
utterance of those who represent us; then it is falling seriously
short of what we expect.

In practice, democracy means different things to different
people. To some, it means the guaranteed right to a roof and a
meal. To others it means the chance, however small, to influence government. To yet others, it may mean a hope that gov-

ernment will represent the best of what we are, because overhanging each government is the threat that it won't be re-elected.

I want to argue that democracy can be something else and something more; not just government by the majority but self-government by all the people; a way of living together in which people genuinely exercise varying degrees of control and responsibility and choose who among them will have authority, and in which the workings of government are limited as much as possible to the rule of law. To some extent, this involves a recovery of what we've lost, of what used to be called civil society before that term was redefined to mean a convocation of socialized robots. It also involves a different understanding of the citizen vis-à-vis the state; a relationship not of dependency but of vigilance.

I have a personal interest in the subject of this book. My grandfather was the fascist leader Sir Oswald Mosley. I grew up with a strong interest in the themes of power and freedom, and in the unhappiness that is unleashed when the pendulum swings towards power. The fascist model of society, committed to a common purpose and led by a messianic defective 'leader' who only feels truly alive when imbued with power, is being aped in many respects by modern democracies. Democratic politics (as they unfold in reality) are not a direct opposite of communism and fascism, but a continuation of the theme of tyranny by the majority, and therefore aptly christened by Mr Blair 'The Third Way.'[1] Politics has become not a conversation about the law to which we citizens must all subscribe, but games of deception, intrigue, management and power.

An electoral majority whose favourite reading is *The Sun*, *Hello!* or *National Enquirer* will obviously deliver a different kind of democracy to one whose favourite reading is Aristotle and Hobbes, even if vocalizing this thought is akin to saying 'I like sex' in a Victorian drawing room. Majorities show a consistent preference for parties and governments who promise to

---

[1]   This parallel was first brought to public attention by Max Beloff, 'Third Way–Third Reich', *The Times*, February 1999.

put right all those miseries and inequalities which used to be laid at God's door. Whereas civil society mitigated or alleviated those ills, governments have done little but exacerbate them, in spite of all their promises. Governments which promise heaven always deliver hell, because the powers they assume in order to deliver heaven create hell. Heaven on earth is, as every religion knows, an impossibility.

The common purpose uniting Western governments is to bring affluence and hide the costs. The costs are to freedom, individuality, diversity, knowledge, understanding, civility, education, art, nature, the simple enjoyment of living and finally to civilization itself. Simple majority democracy lets us all down because however much the majority as individuals may deplore what is happening, they show neither the will nor the understanding to insist that democracy takes another path.

CHAPTER 1

Democracy and its Corruptions

'The one pervading evil of democracy is the tyranny of the majority, or rather of that party, not always the majority, that succeeds, by force or fraud, in carrying elections.' That sentence, so resonant with recent events all over the world and particularly in America, was written by Acton in 1877. The problems with democracy have a long pedigree.

One problem is that democracy has always had two definitions. The first definition is government by and for *all* the people. Since the word democracy means literally 'the people rule,' we may take this to be the true as well as the desirable meaning; but it is hard to implement in practice, because a 'people' will have many different interests, all clamouring to be heard and acted upon. In practice, the only way it can be implemented is for government to remain above and beyond the clamour of different interests; but this is not the route that has been travelled.

The second definition, easier to implement but potentially much less satisfactory, is government by a simple majority. And 'government by majority' is all too apt to degenerate into government by a minority, as disillusioned voters, who feel they are represented by no particular party, drop out of the voting altogether.

Common to all democracies in practice is a law-making body consisting of representatives elected by majority popular vote. If we prefer the more difficult definition of democracy —

government by and for *all* the people — it follows that minorities may require protection from the majority, which may be decent and well-meaning, but equally well may not.

The 'tyranny of the majority' is a phrase used by many writers on democracy since the days of Plato and Aristotle. When the majority seethes with malice towards a minority, it may only be the law that can hold the majority in check; but what protection is that, when the law can be changed or ignored? Tyrannies of a majority can be just as evil as any other kind of tyranny; perhaps even more so, as when a majority sets out to exterminate a minority completely. The frequency of such endeavours will surely be what marks out the twentieth century in history.

Those needing protection may be ethnic or cultural or religious minorities, or they may be a class. The rich have always been vulnerable in a democracy, because the less affluent majority is likely to want their money. The rich were the vulnerable minority under consideration when democracy was written about by the ancient Greeks. Solon, born around 638 BC, was a poet as well as a statesman; his reputation as the founder of democracy rests upon his even-handedness between rich and poor. He recognised that a measured redistribution of wealth is not only necessary for democracy to survive, it is also just. For those who manage to get their hands on large amounts of money are not necessarily the most admirable or the most deserving: 'many curs are rich, while men of principle are poor':

> One man makes noble efforts, but despite them all
>   falls into unforseen calamity:
> Another acts badly, yet God gives him complete success,
>   freed from his folly's consequence.

On the other hand, Solon had no time for demagogues stirring up envy and greed in the populace:

> By their foolishness, the citizens themselves seek to destroy
>   our city's pride,
> Unprincipled mob-leaders — may they suffer badly
>   for their crimes! —
> They know not how to prosper modestly, nor to enjoy in peace
>   the happiness they have.

Known as the 'law-giver,' Solon created the first constitution of Athens, which was designed to maintain a balance of power, and keep both rich and poor from acting tyrannically.

This principle of 'government for the good of all' underpinned the concerns of later Greek philosophers. Aristotle, born 384 BC, described three types of government; rule by one person, rule by a few, and rule by the many. Each type, he said, can exist in a good or a bad manifestation. When one person rules well, he is a monarch; when he rules selfishly, he is a tyrant. Equally, 'the few' can rule well or badly depending on whether they rule selfishly or in the common interest. The same factor determines whether rule by 'the many' is good or bad; does 'the many' want to tyrannize, or does it want to rule wisely and in the best interest of all?

Whatever the virtues and faults of Athenian democracy, we would hardly recognize it as democracy today. Excluded from its citizenship were women, foreign residents and slaves. Acton again:

> A state which has only 30,000 citizens in a population of 500,000, and is governed, practically, by about 3,000 people at a public meeting, is scarcely democratic.

The history of democracy since then has included widening, in fits and starts, the franchise — to include eventually everyone except children, incarcerated criminals and the insane.

The Greek philosophers were generally sceptical, if not positively disapproving, of even their limited form of democracy. Yet by their various criticisms they established the principles which would underpin the successful workings of future democratic states. Socrates encouraged citizens to think for themselves and not take the word of the powerful on trust. Plato insisted that all civil authority should be held in respect of the higher authority of the public good and of the Gods, and so be limited and conditional. And Aristotle in his old age admitted that democracy must have a place in the ideal constitution; that power should be distributed among the citizens according to both property and numbers, so that no class should predominate. His ideal constitution was mixed.

The idea of a mixed constitution essentially adds components to a democracy to protect vulnerable minorities. This makes it less democratic as 'majority democracy', but more democratic as government by and for *all* the people. What components to add has been the subject of debate ever since, and various countries come up with various solutions. In Britain, the debate was rekindled recently in discussions over the composition of the second House, when it was thought no longer suitable that hereditary titles were a proper qualification. A commission was set up to decide on more appropriate criteria and its report recommended that various minorities should be formally recognised and represented in the second chamber. (This has not been implemented by the present government, who appear happier with the current mix of what historian Hugh Bicheno calls 'government placepersons and others having all the attributes of petty criminals save the minimum courage to rob the helpless openly.')

Constitutional additions to protect minorities come under fire from politicians who prefer their power undiluted, and from voters who like simple solutions. In the words of Channing (1780–1842)

> The doctrine that the majority ought to govern passes with the multitude as an intuition, and they have never thought how far it is to be modified in practice and how far the application of it ought to be controlled by other principles.

When politicians appeal for simple majority democracy and begin to absorb all civil institutions into the state, they are paving the way for tyranny – the familiar 'tyranny of the majority'.

Democracy in America

When the American colonists won their freedom after the War of Independence, the most influential among them were sent by their various states to discuss what kind of constitution the new republic should have. There was widespread agreement on two things; the powers of the new federal government vis-à-vis the states should be limited; and majority democracy was the great peril to be avoided.

Washington's concern was to avoid the dangers of party politics and factionalism, in which the tyranny of one party would oppress the rest. Madison agreed: 'In all cases where the majority are united by a common interest or passion the rights of the minority are in danger.' And Hamilton:

> If government is in the hands of the few, they will tyrannize over the many; if in the hands of the many, they will tyrannize over the few. It ought to be in the hands of both, and they should be separated ... Representation alone will not do; demagogues will generally prevail.

There was great apprehension among those who wrote the constitution that it would not serve the purposes for which it was designed, i.e. that it would not protect the people from those waiting to exploit and abuse them. Their apprehensions were well-founded. One by one, their anxieties were fulfilled.

The first to be fulfilled was Washington's, that party politics and factionalism would dominate the affairs of state. The electoral college in particular was designed to resist the influence of party and faction, the idea being that each state should elect its most respected citizens to choose the president. Within ten years, political parties had taken over elections to the electoral college. (The original intention being lost, the electoral college now seems a strange anomaly, whereby a president may be elected on a minority popular vote.)

A second anxiety, that parties on coming to power would dish out favours to the factions which had elected them, was not fulfilled for another twenty or so years. During that time, the interests of the South and the North had diverged, and between 1824 and 1832 pro-Northern interests, riding on the back of widespread popular revulsion against slavery, legislated tariffs which favoured its industrial powerbase over and against that of Southern agriculture. The Civil War was fought as much over this principle as over slavery. Ever since victory of the North over the South, distributing favours among supporters has been the norm for incoming governments.

A third anxiety of the founding fathers was that the US would turn into a scheming imperial power. Towards the end of Washington's farewell address (1796) the following paragraph occurs (it is oddly missing from the version of the text currently posted by the State Department on the internet):

> In offering to you, my countrymen, these counsels of an old and affectionate friend, I dare not hope they will make the strong and lasting impression I could wish; that they will control the usual current of the passions, or prevent our nation from running the course which has hitherto marked the destiny of nations. But, if I may even flatter myself that they may be productive of some partial benefit, some occasional good; that they may now and then recur to moderate the fury of party spirit, to warn against the mischiefs of foreign intrigue, to guard against the impostures of pretended patriotism; this hope will be a full recompense for the solicitude for your welfare, by which they have been dictated.

When the North won the Civil War, the newly powerful central government was tempted to just these mischiefs of foreign intrigue. Seward, the leading spirit among the pro-North, pro-industrial faction, argued to his fellow-countrymen:

> You are already the great continental power of America. But does that content you? I trust it does not. You want the commerce of the world, which is the empire of the world.

How prophetic were his words! And another pattern was thereby established: of a 'fight against evil' being the best opportunity for federal and robber-imperial power to extend itself. This theme will be investigated in a later chapter.

Censorship in America

The great French commentator on America, Alexis de Tocqueville (1805–1859) puzzled over another feature of American democracy which survives to this day; its success at managing dissenting voices, and the lack of any need for formal political censorship.

Every now and then, a great groundswell of popular opinion in America actually succeeds in changing policy, as it did in the Vietnam War. Outside of these occasions, dissent rumbles away and can be published for the most part freely in small-circulation journals. It never even reaches the majority of the public, so there is no need for any authoritarian reaction. There is the further reassurance that even if it does reach a wider audience, public opinion is more robustly conformist in America than anywhere else on earth. Those, for instance, who object to the activities of the CIA in destabilizing foreign countries, financing murder and torture and propping up corrupt regimes are dismissed as irritants or radical crackpots by the majority of voters, who want two things passionately: prosperity, and a belief that America is good. Only when a spectacular outrage shakes the feel-good factor of being American is there any mainstream objection.

Censorship is unnecessary because the mainstream media censor themselves, for commercial not political reasons. 'We give our readers what they want to read' is a principle which applies also to TV, film, and any popular medium. If an item might offend 'consumers' — thereby tainting advertisers and their products with unpatriotic odium, it will not be disseminated.

This genius of American democracy, to make dissent for the most part simply irrelevant, was noted by de Tocqueville in 1835:

> There is no freedom of opinion in America. The ruling power (i.e. the majority) in the United States is not to be made game of. The smallest reproach irritates its sensibility, and the slightest joke that has any foundation in truth renders it indignant; from the forms of its language up to the solid virtues of its character, everything must be made the subject of encomium. No writer, whatever be his eminence, can escape paying this tribute of adulation to his fellow citizens. The majority lives in the perpetual utterance of self-applause, and there are certain truths which the Americans can learn only from strangers or from experience.

He noted that the power of this censorship was more powerful even than the censorship of the European tyrant Louis XIV:

> Labrouyère inhabited the palace of Louis XIV when he composed his chapter on 'The Great', and Molière criticized courtiers in the plays that were acted before the court. But the ruling power in the United States is not to be made game of.

De Tocqueville summed up the attitude of America to its dissidents, shunned and deprived of esteem:

> You are free to think differently from me and to retain your life, your property, and all that you possess; but you are henceforth a stranger among your people. You may retain your civil rights, but they will be useless to you, for you will never be chosen by your fellow citizens if you solicit their votes; and they will affect to scorn you if you ask for their esteem. You will remain among men, but you will be deprived of the rights of mankind. Your fellow creatures will shun you like an impure being; and even those who believe in your innocence will abandon you, lest they should be shunned in their turn. Go in peace! I have given you your life, but it is an existence worse than death.

Since de Tocqueville wrote, the main difference is that there is now a flourishing small industry of dissident writers and publications which are all the more strident and fierce for the impossibility that they will have any influence on the majority.

In between de Tocqueville and today was the case of Mark Twain. During the Cold War, American academics were astonished to hear that Soviet Russia was accusing it of political censorship of its most popular and celebrated writer. Mark Twain, so the accusation went, had spent the last years of his life writing passionately against US imperialism; and these writings had been suppressed.

A little investigation revealed that it was indeed true; he had spent his last years thus, and none of those writings were in print. A little further investigation revealed that the Mark Twain Company, which owned all his writings, was indeed suppressing them; but for commercial reasons, because they would spoil his image as a good American and threaten sales of his work. So a book was allowed to be published to remedy this situation, a compilation of his more acerbic writings under the title *On The Damned Human Race*. The mass public ignored it — the whole affair was a storm in a teacup. The selective attention of the great American complacency was robust.

American democracy today

America is now a democracy ruled by a small minority whose factions — represented by the two parties — diverge only slightly in their interests. Each party regularly hands out favours to the interests which finance it, and central government seizes ever more power over the lives of its citizens. Half those eligible to vote do not bother,[1] so the president is elected by roughly a quarter of eligible voters. Many of those who do vote do it somewhat despairingly, wondering why democracy cannot produce a better choice, often voting more against the other candidate than for their own,[2] so the proportion of real enthusiasts for the president or for particular Senators and Congressmen may be very small indeed.

Who or what is the minority that runs America? Cobbett called America 'an aristocracy of the rich — the most damned of all aristocracies.' The huge amounts of money needed to mount a political campaign exclude all except the rich, with their two party factions. In such circumstances it is patronising cheek to criticize poor people for failing to vote. For whom would they vote? However, two centuries of being ruled by the rich, with the important caveat that they must share it out and please enough of their camp followers to win elections, has helped the country grow very rich indeed, in spite of its enormous foreign debts. Thus, popular dissent is quiet.

Democracy in Europe

Democracy in America developed from English roots under the restraining influence of a constitution. The constitution was designed by conscientious and deliberate thinkers, committed to ideas of liberty and responsible government, in a process of argument and compromise and in the urgent necessity of immediate requirement.

The development of democracy in Europe was quite different. It emerged gradually, making progress by degrees and in constant political struggle with what was already there — the

[1] In 1996, 49% of eligible voters voted; in 2000, a closer and more dramatic election, 51%. Figures for the Senate and Congress are consistently even lower.

[2] For instance, voting *against* Dole because he might tax gasoline; *against* Bush because he would cut social programmes.

ancient system of monarchs, nobles and people. In the old system, a sort of balance existed in that the monarch and people shared a common interest in preventing the nobles from exercising too much power. Also moderating the exercise of power was the principle that the laws of God should hold sway over the laws of man; however much hypocrisy accompanied it, the principle was a significant restraining factor over monarchs, nobles and people alike. Even the church, itself an enormous temporal power, was occasionally restrained by it. Extreme and pervasive tyrannies of the kind common in the twentieth century found it harder to flourish in an age when all agreed that God would punish those who transgressed.

As the educated middle classes became more significant, so pressure grew for representative democracy as we might recognize it today. Middle class demagogues set about persuading the people that the old system was not in their interests. The people themselves were not easily persuaded, for monarchical government provided certain assurances which people were reluctant to abandon. In England for instance, the capricious and overbearing Charles I provoked civil war; but when the parliamentarians won it, they had to suppress simple democracy right from the start, because most of the populace and the elected assembly wanted a return to monarchy. According to the historian Conrad Russell:

> It was impossible to have a republic based on free elections in a predominantly royalist country, in which the king's accession day was still greeted with spontaneous public celebrations.

Cromwell, seeking stability as well as a form of workable democracy, found himself reluctantly adopting more powers that the monarch ever had. When he was asked to take the title of king, the intention of the proposers was to reduce his power, not increase it. Parliament 'knew what a king could do, but not what a protector could do, and the restoration of kingship could mean the restoration of the rule of law.'

In continental Europe, democracy met with more intransigent resistance. Partly in reaction to pressure for democratic change, the theory of the 'enlightened despot' was born. If government were conducted according to reason — as opposed to religion, hierarchy and superstition — then a ruler could rule in the best interests of his people with the help of other 'reasonable' people. Democracy would never be necessary; in fact it would be counterproductive, because 'the people' were in the nature of things less reasonable and less educated than the mixture of philosophers and bureaucrats whom the monarch would choose to administer them.

Using reason and unlimited power, a well-meaning despot could, so the theory went, maximize the happiness of all, exercising a maximum of power and control over the lives and institutions of his subjects. This new rationalist justification of tyranny would be later adopted by revolutionary political movements inclined to claim absolute power for the state, to be exercised on behalf of 'the masses' by self-appointed enlightened representatives, who would — of course — be the revolutionaries themselves.

The first victorious attempt at democratic revolution, the French Revolution, collapsed in disorder. It had been inspired by the example of America, but in the chaos which ensued those who wished to adopt a new constitution were defeated by political manipulators and demagogues. As a result, first France then Europe was turned into a bloodbath.

The example of the French Revolution haunted attempts at democracy in Europe for a century and a half. In the meantime, industrialization was giving power to a new class, for whom exploitation of large numbers of depersonalized workers was just part of the industrial process. So a further new class was born, the industrial proletariat, whose degrading living and working conditions became the scandal of European civilization.

'The masses — what masses?'

'Anyone taken as an individual is tolerably sensible and reasonable; as a member of a crowd he becomes a blockhead.' Such is Schiller's explanation for the behaviour of people *en masse*, doing things they would never do as individuals.

In the nineteenth century the term 'the masses' was coined to denote the new aggregations of industrial workers living in penury and desperation around the new factories of mass-production. Their desperate situation and their concentration in small areas made them ideal material for revolutionaries to work on. What way forward did they have in the old order of things? What else but total upheaval could better their condition?

The answer to these questions in England was 'organized labour,' which gradually became possible by changes in the law, but on the Continent the tradition of enlightened despotism put up a more brutal resistance to trades unions and to self-organizing labour.

Meanwhile liberals, seeing the injustice and the oppression in the situation, took up the cause of the workers, and conservative Europeans became nervous about the consequences. Burckhardt wrote to a friend in the 1880's:

> Everything is possible in Europe since the Paris Commune, chiefly because there are everywhere good, splendid liberal people who do not quite know the boundaries of right and wrong and where the duty of resistance and defence begins. It is these men who open the doors and level the paths for the terrible masses everywhere.

Opposing attitudes to 'the masses' put intellectuals into many different camps, and between them a battleground of ideas which remains alive to this day.

One camp insists that even to think of large numbers of people as a 'mass' is to dehumanize them and thereby pave the way for mass murder. John Carey wrote, in *The Intellectuals and the Masses*:

> Contemplating the extermination of the Jews was made easier by thinking of them as a mass ... In this sense the Holocaust may be seen as the ultimate indictment of the idea of the mass and its acceptance by twentieth-century intellectuals.

The twentieth century intellectuals of whom John Carey disapproves saw 'the masses' as repulsive and vulgar, deadly to culture, swarming insects, faceless worker-robots, ineducable, stupid; or even like a mass phalanx of the walking dead, as in a modern computer game. T.S. Eliot's line from *The Wasteland* on people walking to work across London Bridge — 'I had not known death had undone so many' — compares the masses, by stealing a line from Dante's inferno, to those already in hell.

The philosopher Michael Oakeshott had a milder version: the 'masses' are those who find it hard to thrive in an individualist world, who long for a sense of belonging and community, and who therefore look to the state for protection and also to tell them what to do. Furthermore each of us, to varying degrees, contains this element of anti-individual or individual *manqué* who wishes the state to be (in Freudian, not Oakeshottian, terms) a gigantic breast, nappy-changer and authority figure, all rolled into one. The state remade in this image is what is popularly called the nanny state, though wet-nurse state or even Mummy-and-Daddy state might be more appropriate.

A less sympathetic view comes from the biologist C.D. Darlington, who wrote objectively of humanity as if it were another species. Upon the subject of political control being removed from the professional classes and given to the masses, he wrote:

> The twentieth century, we were told in 1905, was going to be the century of the common man, and so it turned out to be. It was devoted to submerging impartially nature and civilization, art and individuality, under the festering sores of economic growth.

Yet another camp, the middle class demagogue-intellectuals, sensed the possibilities of power latent in the masses for a new class war in which they could be leaders. They tended to see the masses in mystical terms, as humanity writ large; the 'people' or the 'proletariat' in whose name they would establish a new millennium. The fulfilment of the individual in this new order would be not the cultivation of his own personality, but according to Fabians like the Webbs: 'the filling, in the best possible way, of his humble function in the great social machine.' Where and when these middle class revolutionaries succeeded in persuading 'the masses' to revolution, they proved to be more ruthless and adept at oppressing them than the old order; but that is another story. The point here is that democracy now had another competitor besides the old order; it had to compete with revolution, with the idea that slaughter and appropriation could lead the way forward to a new age of happiness and prosperity.

The revolutions inspired by these writers and orators are now a matter of history. The most terrible century of all has left us; the mass movements inspired by intellectuals have done their worst; the piles of dead, the burnings the shootings and gassings even worse than the slaughters of Genghis Khan and Tamburlane. Whether the destruction of European civilization will be as profound as the destruction of Eastern civilization wreaked by those two men remains to be seen.

From all this, democracy emerged as the only realistic option. Criticism of the fundamental idea was henceforth irrelevant. 'The masses', or the people, the majority, are now in charge. They are affluent, educated by the state of which they are masters, and in these circumstances they have proved to be not malicious. This fits with Edmund Burke's observation:

> the people have no interest in disorder. When they do wrong, it is their error and not their crime. But with the governing part of the state, it is far otherwise. They may certainly act ill by design, as well as by mistake.

From this perspective, the most pertinent accusation levelled against electorates in modern democracies is gullibility. They believe the promises of rascals and of an even more dangerous type, the messianic self-believer. For a politician to be in with a chance of election he must be prepared to make false promises. From this comes the deterioration in political life, as it empties of honest men and women. The electorate may be guilty only of gullibility, but it is gullibility on a massive scale, capable of reducing the status of citizens to state- and corporate-owned serfs, and of turning the planet into a desert.

But there is another account implicit in the above, which is this. Human civilization has prospered first and foremost by the achievements of a few of its members, scattered individuals who, like Pushkin, arise out of unpredictable combination into propitious circumstances. The stability of society is provided by those with talent but no genius who carry forward what is valuable in civilization. The vast numbers of humanity whom civilization now supports have flourished in the wake of the abilities, inventions and ideas of these others, including ideas of governance and freedom. The masses and their unscrupulous leaders have created and won a class war which leaves them in charge, and this unholy collusion is now reshaping the world in its own interests and in its own image. Distrustful and misunderstanding of the conditions of freedom and responsibility, only able truly to enjoy 'bread and circuses' — that is affluence, entertainment and power — the majority and their leaders offer a choice to talented individuals: find yourself employment in the provision of bread and circuses, or find yourself ignored.

The situation is exacerbated because in each one of us to varying degrees there exists the indivdual *manqué* referred to above, who wishes to be looked after and handed Paradise on a plate. Whereas this powerful persona used to be expressed — and the hopelessness of its condition felt — in religion, it now looks fully expectant to the state for the impossible fulfilment of its needs.

In this account, the truth of which is uncertain because the drama is not yet played out, items such as 'freedom of speech' and institutions such as the environmentalist charities exist as tokens of conscience, acquitting the sentimental majority in its own eyes of any wrongdoing. Meanwhile the actual and vicious business of suppressing freedom and conscience and plundering the planet carries on abated, and our productivist society continues to supply us with all the shoddy paraphernalia we are so familiar with, delivered by corporations and governments where sense, conscience and responsibility are alike absent. This is the form of totalitarianism represented in Britain as the 'Third Way' and in the United States as the 'New World Order.'

The heart of darkness in this tale is that the majority in all civilized countries now actively prefers this arrangement to any condition of responsible freedom. Civilization to the majority means principally a source of goods, novelties, services and comforts. Their political leaders reassure them there is no need for restraint; their favoured courtiers, masquerading as intellectuals, academics and creative types, supply them with an endless supply of flattery. Just as the Greek love of war is reputed to have destroyed that civilization, so the blind love affair of the majority — a majority that is in all of us — with its own comforts and stimulations is destroying ours.

The irony seems rather bitter when one reflects that the whole glorious endeavour of civilization is being destroyed without a great deal of pleasure being had by anyone.

Times of plenty

In theory, with machines making so much wealth for us, we should all be able to sit back and enjoy ourselves a bit. That was how it seemed to the science fiction writers of the 1950s; by the year 2000 we would all be dressed in aluminium suits and travelling around on monorails. Our leisure time was a bit of a puzzle — what would such lofty creatures do for fun? But in reality that problem didn't arise. People with time on their hands are searching for another job; and those with jobs work longer and longer hours.

Mechanization has transformed all our relations — with each other, with the natural world, with work and production — in ways we have yet to understand. One side-effect of the prosperity we now enjoy was described by Willa Cather in a novel written in 1925:

> With prosperity came a kind of callousness; everyone wanted to destroy the old things they used to take pride in. The orchards, which had been nursed and tended so carefully twenty years ago, were now left to die of neglect. It was less trouble to run into town in an automobile and buy fruit than it was to raise it.

Overproduction is most clearly evident in the fact that war is now good for economies not for the old-fashioned reason of plunder, but because it stimulates production at home. 'America's defence spending,' according to *The Times* (Aug 1st 2003), 'grew so strongly in supplying the war against Iraq that it propelled the US economy to a spring surge.' In other words, production of goods (tanks, missiles, ammunition etc) destined only to be destroyed or to become redundant is good for the economy. On the face of it, to avoid unnecessary bloodshed, it might be better for the government just to pay manufacturers to make stuff and smash it up. More simply still, it could adopt Keynes's suggestion and distribute money to those most likely to spend it, the poor.[3]

As far as democracy is concerned, the emancipation of the majority from skilled hands-on labour, most of which is now undertaken by machines, has resulted in a large number of people available for other work. Two expanding concerns have been happy to make use of this work force: corporations and governments. Corporations manage the machines that make us wealthy, and also the wealth that is thereby created. With that wealth electorates can afford states employing a quarter of the workforce and absorbing half of all gross national product — which is roughly the situation in most Western democracies.

Our huge democratic manager-states are not as tyrannical as their forebears — the communist and fascist states — but they borrow many of their techniques and they share common origins, which is why I have made communism and fascism the subject of the next chapter.

---

[3] Keynes's actual suggestion, included in his *General Theory*, was this: 'If the Treasury were to fill old bottles with bank notes, bury them at suitable depths in disused coal mines which are then filled up with town rubbish, and leave them to private enterprise on the well-tried principles of *laissez faire* to dig them up again, there need be no more unemployment and, with the help of the repercussions, the real income of the community and its capital wealth also would probably become a great deal greater than it actually is.' Whether the money and/or bottles would ever reach the holes, let alone the poor who would actually spend it — that being the point of the exercise — seems not to have been addressed. My thanks to N.M. and R.S. for this information.

Chapter 2

Communism and Fascism

With industrialization came a huge increase in overall wealth and a corresponding increase in class exploitation. It was manifestly unfair that a few capitalists should control almost all the wealth created by the new industrial processes, especially when workers in their factories were living off bare subsistence wages and working long hours in terrible conditions. Moreover, the easy alliance of the new industrialists with the old ruling classes gave the working class no hope that their lot would improve without struggle.

The main advocate for total revolution was Karl Marx. He constructed a huge theoretical argument, drawing on the work of contemporary thinkers such as Darwin, Ricardo and Hegel, to justify a promise that revolution would install a proletarian paradise on earth. An initial period of total control by the party would be followed by the withering away of the state. There would then be a classless society with no exploitation and therefore social harmony — 'prehistory will be at an end, history will begin.'

A belief in magic would seem, in retrospect, necessary to go along with such a programme, or at least a strong variety of faith. In that respect Marxism was like a religion; but Marxism was not a religion, it was a programme for building paradise on earth. Most religions modestly and wisely content themselves with locating paradise somewhere — or sometime — else.

The revolutionaries who took over Russia in 1917 were in no doubt that violence was needed to implement their vision, and so the killings began. The killings went on and paradise never came. Many of those who had believed the stories of paradise were themselves killed as the revolution progressed. The state took over central planning of the economy — the result was shortages and starvation. The state took control of science — the result was scientists murdered and replaced with quacks. The state took over the arts — the result was dead artists and bad art. Etcetera. And so it went on until the state — three generations later — was forced to withdraw and again allow some degree of human freedom.

Unlike communism, fascism arrived without preparation, with no baggage of theory, no great body of justifying literature to announce it. It arrived more-or-less on the tide of the moment, the 'inspired creation' of Mussolini, a journalist-cum-political agitator, who combined the enthusiasms of socialism and nationalism with the pragmatism of achieving power by violence. 'Fascism is not a dogma but an opportunity,' he said.

Fascism has its opportunity when the conditions of life become a lot worse than usual. When economic collapse and social disorder hit a country which is used to a fair degree of order and prosperity, people contemplate desperate measures for putting the world to rights. In Italy, even more than economic collapse and social disorder, the condition which allowed fascism to seize control was the extent to which organized groups were resorting to violence without any serious retribution from the state. Democracy was failing to maintain its authority, as it would later fail in Germany. Sympathy for one or other of the armed groups plaguing everyday life — fascists, socialists, anarchists, communists, monarchists — was in many individuals stronger than loyalty to the government of the day, even among those whose job it was to enforce the law. As a result, the law was often not enforced.

The *fascii*, from which the word 'fascism' originates, were 'bundles' of violent men roaming the countryside and beating up or killing those they disapproved of. But, said the fascists, they had a justification for all this: a vision of an Italy that would be worthy of its ancestors. Under their leadership Italy would regain its days of greatness; the days when it was the jewel in the crown of civilization, the days of Petrarch and Dante, of splendid achievements in philosophy and the arts and in warfare. Machiavelli, who would have turned in his grave at the crude and vulgar antics of the fascists, was hailed as the prophet of the new state.

Unlike the socialists, who were committed to class war, the fascists promised an Italy where the different classes would unite under the one banner of seeking a great national future. Supporters of fascism came from many walks of life — intellectuals, artists, businessmen, workers from both town and country, the dispossessed; *petit bourgeois* lovers of order as well as mere adventurers getting on a bandwagon. Underpinning the whole operation were those who actually went out and used violence — the familiar fascist thugs, ill-educated men relieving their feelings of inadequacy by exercising physical power over others.

The price to be paid for the implemention of the 'heroic destiny' of the fascists was the elimination of its enemies; but this was no more than justice in the national interest. Moreover, it was a price that would be paid by others. Turning a blind eye to the ugliness was all that was required of the populace at large. So, the killings started. The 'vision' and 'heroic destiny' became no more than repeated celebrations of the power of the fascist state. There being no individual freedom, there was nothing else to celebrate.

Meanwhile every idea which had ever inspired humanity was corrupted in the service of the fascist state. Ideas noble in the service of freedom became squalid and evil put to use as instruments of the state. Patriotism, authority, heroism, education, science, law, philosophy, art, endeavour — all were transformed into instruments of a narrow vision of power. Fascism demonstrated supremely, 'The corruption of the best is the worst.'

The totalitarian state

Once a totalitarian state is established, it exercises an absolute and quixotic authority over everything, so there is great advantage to be gained by allying oneself to it and everything to lose by not so doing. To maintain an aloofness is to invite censure and exclusion; to oppose the state is to risk annihilation. Anyone in public office whose integrity prevents him from becoming a fellow-traveller is replaced by an ambitious camp-follower.

These states have been called 'criminal' in that they transgress the essential element of law, which is to be impartial. In a fascist state, as in a communist (and also, as I will argue later, to some extent in a modern corporate state) the law is no longer impartial; it is something rewritten at will to enact 'policy', favouring now this group, now that, demonstrating the power of its masters to make or break lives. The kind of character who rises to the top in a criminal state is unscrupulous, positively vengeful against any challenge, and envious of the moral superiority of all it has displaced or murdered. This culture of fearful and vicious mediocrity has been observed in all forms of totalitarian society, permeating the organs of administration and control[1].

The great national purpose, whether communist or fascist, was vested in the person of one man, under whom bureaucracy would (supposedly) be not a dead weight but an instrument of progress. The head of the state would no longer be a mere 'ruler' applying the law with a sense of old-fashioned justice; he would be a 'leader,' taking his people forward to a bright new future. Moreover, the 'will of the people' would be elevated above considerations of mere morality and justice and be the guiding principle of the state. And, of course, the will of the people would be interpreted as well as fulfilled by the leader.

With hindsight it is obvious that the greatness of these totalitarian visions never came about. In their place came butchery and devastation of varying magnitudes, up to and including

---

[1]   See for instance the memoirs of Nadezhda Mandelstam, *Hope Against Hope* and *Hope Abandoned;* also those of George Faludy.

the evils of Stalin's Russia and Hitler's Germany. Why did the promises turn out to be so false? The promise, after all, was simple enough: 'Give all power to us, and we will use it to build a paradise for you on earth.'

We might counter this question with another question: With the whole weight of the tradition of Western civilization crying out that it's a bad idea to give unlimited power to anyone, much as an audience shouts 'Look behind you!' to an innocent in a pantomime, why did Everyman walk into the trap?

The answers to the second question are still relevant today. With mass democracy came the determining influence of a majority uneducated in, therefore unprotective of, the liberal tradition. State education had already placed literacy and numeracy and other 'useful' skills at the top of the list of priorities. It was — and still is — nowhere in the state's interests to educate citizens in a genuinely liberal (as opposed to a managerial liberal) tradition. Secondly, alongside the growth of democracy was the development of an intellectual tradition counter to the liberal tradition, holding that a strong state was a good thing; government could and should take control of the affairs of its citizens in the name of the common good. It was this ideology that state education tended to promote.

The enlightened despots of the eighteenth century found two justifications for taking absolute power over their citizens. One was religious, the 'divine right of kings.' Kings were chosen by God to personify His rule on Earth. The other was scientific and rationalist; the monarch would choose educated and wise administrators who would know what was in the best interests of citizens. The rule of the enlightened despots, while tyrannical and absolute, was not marked by millions of dead among their own citizens. For one thing, God was for them a given reality and God disapproved of unnecessary slaughter; but they were also restrained by their own inclinations as human individuals. The enjoyment of power for its own sake was tempered by enjoyment of its fruits, the noble amusements of hunting and warfare and patronage. Exterminating swathes of the citizenry was not on the agenda as it had been earlier in religious wars,[2] and as it would be later when self-styled representatives of 'the people' would take over as absolute despots.

In political terms, a recognition of the authority of God does not distinguish between whether God 'exists' or is a symbol of the superior and uncompromising power of Nature imposing limits upon what we can and can't get away with. But once this God is no longer recognized, the possibilities of human folly as well as human crime lose all limits. When absolute power is granted to, or seized by, a person and an organization, what follows depends on the nature of the person and the culture of the organization. Everyone and everything (except their own eventual demise) is suddenly within their power. To make things worse, a system of total power, once set up, is vulnerable to exploitation by other operators possibly even less scrupulous than those who set it up. This occurred, for example, when Stalin took over from Lenin in Soviet Russia.

An interesting question is, why should such a system of total power and social control ever come to an end? Hitler's demise in his bunker, his thousand-year dream destroyed by foreign armies, was uncharacteristic of twentieth-century despots, most of whom died in their beds. What brings horror to an end seems more often to be a mere running out of steam: evil finally gluts itself. In the Soviet Union, those who replenished the system were eventually either drunk and incompetent or keen to see the evil come to an end; the 'evil empire' had lost its power to command and coerce. (The aggressions of the American superpower, which likes to think it brought the Soviet Union down by attrition, on the contrary kept it going after Stalin's death by uniting the country in military effort.)

The role of the intellectuals

The crimes committed by Nazis and communists defy comparison with anything that occurred before in human history, except perhaps the assaults on settled civilization by the

---

[2] For instance, when Luther sanctioned the extermination of Catholic peasants in 1525 with the words 'let everyone who can smite, slay and stab the peasants secretly and openly.'

Mongols. The culture of a ruling class that for instance, as occurred in Romania, regularly got drunk and had sexual intercourse with chained-up infants, is not a phenomenon which is known to have existed before except in the isolated activities of psychopaths such as the fifteenth century Gilles de Rais and his assistants — and he has haunted the imagination of Europe ever since as 'Bluebeard'.

The elevation of the beast in humanity has been blamed by many cultural commentators on intellectuals.[3] 'The intellectual leaders of the peoples have produced and propagated the fallacies which are on the point of destroying liberty and Western civilization,' wrote the economist von Mises in 1947. 'The intellectuals alone are responsible for the mass slaughters which are the characteristic mark of our century. They alone can reverse the trend and pave the way for a resurrection of freedom.'

Von Mises had in mind intellectuals who propagated totalitarian ideas regardless of how dishonest, irresponsible and badly thought-out they were. There were many attractions for an intellectual in joining a revolutionary political movement. Perhaps strongest of all was a feeling of being one of a 'community of the righteous', one of the good people, championing the underdog and helping implement social justice. There were also other more mundane attractions — such as instant readerships, pay cheques and power.[4]

The number of fascist and communist intellectuals has since dwindled in the wake of their crimes. But the moral ideas used to justify their crimes are alive and well today. For the communists, the slogan was 'the end justifies the means.' The idea — born long before the communists — is that acts normally considered criminal can be justified if they are in 'the common good'. This principle is ubiquitously used by governments

---

[3]   One such intellectual, George Bataille, wrote a book glorifying the crimes of Gilles de Rais.

[4]   The audience at a recent London conference, bemoaning the loss of influence of intellectuals in public life, was surprised to hear from one of the more distinguished political scientists on the panel that this was because academics, intellectuals and other theoreticians have for the most part been wrong about just about everything when they have attempted to influence the development of public policy.

today, justifying activities such as appropriating land for road-building, monitoring our daily movements and selling arms.

The fascists came from a different angle to arrive at the same place. For them, morality and law were bourgeois and contemptible unless they served (their) higher purpose. Nothing was forbidden so long as it brought forward their new heroic destiny for humankind.

The idea that moral and legal restraints are secondary, that we can as states or individuals elect a 'higher purpose' which makes them redundant, needed a theorist of course, and for the modern age that theorist was Nietzsche. The whole hotbed of revolutionary moral and intellectual Europe was alive with such ideas, but Nietzsche made it his life's work to elaborate them and what he thought would be their consequences. Fundamental to a justification of fascism, for instance, was the Nietzschean idea of the *ubermensch* – superman – who is 'no longer affected by pity, suffering, tolerance of the weak.' By self-knowledge, he has earned the right of escape from traditional moral scruples. The *ubermensch* may break boundaries and moral constraints at will, because he is to humans what humans are to the apes. 'Man is something that shall be surpassed. What is the ape to man? A laughingstock or a painful embarrassment. And man shall be just that to the superman: a laughingstock, a painful embarrassment.'

Fascism turned the idea of the *ubermensch* into a political opportunity. Human virtues of compassion, restraint, and justice were replaced with Superman virtues of contempt, acting on impulse, and the will to power. The idea that political or artistic or merely individual fufilment must involve the breaking of moral bounds was elevated into a cult of transgression, taken over by the state, which still animates our civilization today. This is another example of *corruptio optimi pessima* – the corruption of the best is the worst. For there is no doubt that great deeds involve transgressions, and the spirit of transgression itself is both beautiful and noble when it moves for freedom and against power. But to suborn this spirit into a doctrine of state power is to corrupt it utterly. The true spirit of transgression here would be to destroy the state. Equally, for individuals to say, 'I will transgress in the interests of becoming great' is not only to put the cart before the horse, but a poor excuse to indulge in personal versions of power and betrayal.

Fascism and communism differed in their rallying cries; the one, heroism and order; the other, equality and fairness. But they both led to the same political reality: dictatorship, with an apparatus of total control and the habitual use of extreme violence. Nor did the sum total of violence used depend on whether they were fascist or communist; at one end of the spectrum are Hitler and Stalin; at the other Franco and Castro.

When fascism had done its worst, it left a Europe stunned by its legacy. Democracy was certainly the wiser in one sense, in that the consequences of voting for the politics of hatred were clear for all to see. But when, some years later, light from the West began to filter through the Iron Curtain, it seemed to surviving dissidents in the Soviet Union — Solzhenitsyn and Nadezhda Mandelstam for instance — that the West was going down the same route, only voluntarily, not by coercion. The huge corporate powers of business and government on the one hand, and a corresponding loss of personal moral responsibility on the other, were making in the West a materialism every bit as deadly to human civilization as that which had been dominating life in the Soviet Union.

CHAPTER 3

Corporations and the Corporate State

It's often assumed that corporations are a product of the 'free market', creatures of nature that like Topsy 'jes' grew'. In fact, nothing could be further from the truth. They are set up, protected, and given special legal status by particular human laws.

A corporation is a group of people drawn together in a common purpose and given a single legal identity. It is an old idea: corporations were recognized in Roman law, mostly for charitable and educational bodies, but also for trade. A corporation is often described as an 'artificial person'. It can own property, in which individual members of the corporation have no rights. It can also owe money which individual corporators have no obligation to pay.

For charitable bodies in particular, corporate status had definite and innocent advantages. An incorporated charity could own gifts made to it by individuals, which could then be protected from misappropriation or misuse. Its continued existence was not dependent upon any one person; it could outlive all of its original members. Its special status in law was justified by its being clearly beneficial to the rest of society. It was as charitable and 'public service' bodies that corporations appeared again in the Middle Ages — town boroughs, ecclesiastical and educational bodies.

Corporations trading for profit also have an old history, mostly connected with the granting of monopoly privileges. These were always an object of distrust and suspicion, both from the sovereign authority that authorised their existence and from everyone else. The suspicions were twofold; one, they might be abusing their monopoly privilege and making too much money; two, they might be doing horrid things in their search for profit. For corporations were necessarily small governments in themselves, with their own rules designed for the pursuit of profit and not as a rule of law.

Adam Smith (1723–90) noted that in his day, trading corporations — 'joint stock companies' — generally failed when they had to compete with partnerships or 'private adventurers' because their managers and employees would be sloppy, inefficient and careless of money which was not their own. Private adventurers, on the other hand, were thorough and vigilant, because their own money was at stake. For this reason, trading corporations generally only prospered while they had a monopoly. The monopoly was usually granted for a limited duration and for a specific purpose, normally to exploit an opportunity which would not be met in the open market such as 'to establish a new trade with some remote and barbarous nation.' Such a monopoly would be in the national interest, Smith wrote, because it would establish a general advantage in trade with that nation. After the expiry of its monopoly the corporation would have to compete with other traders, and: 'without a monopoly, it would appear from experience, a joint stock company cannot long carry on any branch of foreign trade.'

There were certain exceptions to this general uncompetitiveness of corporations, Adam Smith noted. One exception was when such huge amounts of capital were needed that a joint stock offer was the only way to raise it; another exception was businesses such as insurance and banking, where 'the operations are capable of being reduced to what is called a Routine.'

The huge growth since Adam Smith's day of the market share of corporations has to do with many factors. His own observations hint at two. Firstly, the amounts of capital needed in international business have grown enormously. Secondly, techniques developed in business schools and programmes of innovative 'business studies' have successfully reduced almost all activity — even innovation — to routinised procedures.

A third factor favouring corporations is their now ubiquitous 'limited liability' — unheard of in Adam Smith's time but recognized in English law in 1858 — which limits the personal liability of investors to what they have actually invested in the company. This of course makes it much less alarming for investors — and it weighs the scales heavily in the favour of corporations when it comes to raising money. Now most 'private adventurers' in fact trade through their own or part-owned corporations to make use of this privilege.

These advantages counter to some extent the fact that large corporations seem to be just as inefficient as they were in Adam Smith's day. A study undertaken in one large corporation recently indicated that 80 per cent of senior management's time was taken up dealing with internal memos. Vastly overblown self-awarded salaries and expenses are another factor reducing their competitiveness.

But there are still further advantages enjoyed by corporations which help outweigh these inefficiencies. Small corporations can behave extremely ruthlessly; they can appear and disappear having defrauded shareholders, workforce and creditors alike — as one banker told me, they 'liquidate, shut down, f__k off and start up under a different name.' Large corporations, on the other hand, enjoy advantages of size. Often-observed habits include: bullying small suppliers and labour markets; using foul play to push out smaller competitors; establishing agreements with other manufacturers to fix prices; using their status as multinationals to relocate across borders to gain advantages — including subsidy payments from the new host; 'creative' use of tax havens and other suspect financial instruments; avoidance of public scrutiny by choosing where they are incorporated; and corruptly influencing governments into granting them covert monopolies. Furthermore, multinational corporations may relocate to a nation where the law is sympathetic or utterly ineffectual — or to where they can pay off law-enforcement agencies and so act criminally with impunity.

Though this list is not exhaustive, and maybe not even very informative (given its familiarity), it does point to one overriding factor: corporations are more effective in being less scrupulous. In other words, they do not compete in markets so much as corner them. A recent defence put up by bosses of Elf Aquitaine, the French oil giant, against charges of corporate and government corruption (in which shareholders and taxpayers were defrauded of hundreds of millions of dollars) was that whole system is so corrupt, the defendants were actually its victims! This might seem to rival the old Yiddish definition of chutzpah, in which a man convicted of murdering his parents pleads to the court for mercy on account of his being an orphan. But meanwhile, the investigating magistrates were under round-the-clock police protection due to the threat of murder by state operatives[1]. A Nazi-style corporate state had, it seems, embedded itself in the democracy.

The habit of moving money around the world to evade regulation and scrutiny makes it hard for investigators to find out what is going on — even during a criminal investigation. Ordinary regulatory bodies simply haven't the resources to find out what is going on financially within and between corporations; but that is mostly irrelevant anyway, because the processes of public scrutiny and review which used to accompany charters of incorporation have largely fallen by the wayside. In the United States, different states competed to attract corporations during the second half of the nineteenth century by making their licensing laws ever more liberal. Further extensions of corporate privilege have since then been sought and given federally; for instance, an 1886 decision by the Supreme Court gave corporations rights to protection under the Fourteenth Amendment, as if they were human persons. Since then, corporations have been claiming more and more rights of privacy and protection under the constitution and its amendments, as if they were vulnerable human creatures of flesh-and-blood.

---

[1] The events are narrated in a book by the investigating magistrate, Eva Joly, *Est-ce dans ce monde-là que nous voulons vivre?*

The position of corporations is now dominant in the market place (though their protected existence makes the market-place anything but free), and individual traders and partnerships are confined to niche markets. Most people, apart from anti-globalization campaigners and environmentalists, now assume that corporations act hugely in the public benefit. Judged purely on the basis of their ability to sequester the wealth of the world, this judgement is no doubt correct. But on any other basis such an assumption is hard to justify. The power of corporations is out of control and democratic majorities seem quite uninterested in the task of limiting it. Most of the media are owned by corporations and this influences what information gets through to the public. The public themselves are mostly employed by corporations; and as Nadezhda Mandelstam said in the context of Soviet Russia, 'if you receive your daily bread from the powers that be, and you want to be in with a chance of getting that little bit extra, then you are wise to give up thinking altogether.'

There is no sign of any election-turning revulsion among voters, even where corporate malfeasance includes murder of decent people by state operatives. Berlusconi in Italy makes laws to protect himself without great loss of popular support. 'Liberty has lost its spell; and democracy maintains itself by the promise of substantial gifts to the masses of the people.' The law is widely regarded among the corporate élite as a *jeu de dupes*, a game for simpletons.

In order to understand this phenomenon, it is not necessary to believe in the universal baseness of human character, nor even in the universal baseness of the rich. It arises out of the culture favoured within corporations. This in turn arises out of the legal duty of corporations, which is simple: to maximize profits for their shareholders. Because of this primary obligation, quite at odds with both law and morality, a corporation is legally obliged to avoid any civility or scruple which gets in the way of profit. From the simplest civilities like, for instance, paying on time, to exercising moral scruples about what they produce — cluster bombs, napalm, rip-off financial instruments, planned-obsolescent goods, environmental destruction etc. — corporate employees must observe no scruple that is legally avoidable.

Suspension of personal moral standards is a requirement for admission to the world of corporate culture and corporate rules-of-play must be adopted in their stead. Adopting a temporary code like this is no problem for most of us; we do it every time we play a game. Within the rules of the game we play ruthlessly; and knowing a game is a game, we expect our competitors to like us afterwards. But, just as those who treat a game as if it were real life destroy the value of the game, so those who treat real life as a game destroy the value of living.

The corporate game picks up lives and transforms them. Dreams are lost in squalid nightmares. Most lawyers now earn their living from advising corporate clients how to avoid the law.

The final advantage enjoyed by corporations is their limited liability in terms of justice. If a corporation is found guilty of a crime, only a fine is practicable. Although a corporation is legally a person, never, I think, has a corporation been jailed. Individuals within corporations are occasionally jailed; but only for defrauding the shareholders, never for illegal dealings vis-à-vis workforces, consumers, corrupted governments abroad, monopolies, pollutions, failure to keep to contracts, defrauding vulnerable parties, etc. There are great difficulties for flesh-and-blood victims in taking a corporation to court — the huge costs of litigation, the uncertainty of where prosecution can or should take place, and the lack of effective international law.

Most publicly-aired objections to the power of corporations, big and small, are linked to the idea that if they were more 'democratically accountable' their abuses of power would stop. But abuses and power are inseparable (when they are not identical) — the only way of reducing abuses is to reduce power. Democracies have been inclined to hand more and more power to corporations and to the state; corporate power and democracy have grown and flourished side by side. There is no sign that proposals to restrict corporate power appeal to the majority of voters. On the contrary, even the most elementary suggestions of limiting corporate misbehaviour — such as abolishing the right of corporations to invest in one another, which would kill most criminal corporate activity at a stroke — have fallen out of memory, so little relevant are they to the democratic world we live in.

That the corporate world and the corporate mentality flourish hand-in-hand with democracy is evident in the growth of the other great corporate entities of our age, which work closely hand-in-hand with the corporations: the corporate 'democratic' state.

The corporate state

The corporate state is a state-with-a-purpose. It has moved beyond its traditional roles of keeping the peace, maintaining the currency, diplomacy and defence. In addition it offers 'management solutions' to the electorate, which require more and more money and power to carry them out. It offers to fix education, health, transport, culture, the environment, health and safety, the arts, agriculture and science. It promises to 'abolish poverty' (though in truth it merely monitors the poor and feeds them at subsistence level). Most important of all — for come election time, this is what candidates are most encouraged to talk about — it promises to make all of us more prosperous.

Fascism and communism produced extreme versions of the corporate state. They were extreme in their promises, extreme in the control they exerted, and extreme in their disappointments. They arrived suddenly, and almost as suddenly they were gone. But the models they devised and developed of a corporate state are still with us. Certain elements of the socialist model have become somewhat discredited, for instance state ownership of industry, and elements of outright coercion in both have mostly been abandoned. Instead, the promises of social management are re-negotiated every few years with the electorate and so they gain the authority of being 'what the people want'.

In the fascist model of the corporate state, society is a network of industrial enterprises. Mussolini's *corporativismo* organized state and industry into one corporate whole. Twenty-two corporations, each representing a branch of 'industry' (including for instance banking, theatre and hotels) were organized and supervised by a national 'Council of Corporations.' This council became the legislative body of the state, making laws primarily in the interests of public prosperity. Corporations operated in free competition within these legal guidelines.

Modern democratic states are moving in the direction of this model, as the state adopts a supervisory role over areas of human activity re-defined as 'industries' — the theatre industry, the tourist industry, the countryside industry etc. The modern corporate state arrives slowly and by degrees. It moves in on the freedom of others with our consent, then with the consent of others it moves in on ours. Like lobsters being cooked, we do not know we are in hot water till it is too late. Besides, the hot water has its comforts: the state will at least keep us from destitution. And the temperature is not entirely unresponsive to our wishes; it shifts lower when we protest, but then always higher again as we become accustomed to the new degree of heat. The heat, of course, is the state taking control of things and leaving us with less freedom (and less income). At the extreme other end of the spectrum would be a state which lets us get on with our lives provided we do not commit murder, robbery etc.

Michael Oakeshott has done most to develop the distinction between these two opposite understandings of what a state should or might be. The latter he calls 'civil association'. The citizens in such a state have only one concern in common, which is to 'act justly'; to obey the law, which itself can be changed as our understandings change of 'what is just'. Citizens need no state-granted 'rights'. They are free to do as they wish in accordance with conditions set by law.

The other notion is 'of a state as an all-embracing, compulsory corporate association and of its government as the manager of an enterprise.' In this kind of state, the citizens are joined in common pursuit of one or more purposes, and legislation is passed to further those purposes. The government does not make laws so much as 'policy'. A citizen is bound to the common purposes. He can't opt out, because the state takes his money and uses it for the common purposes, and because the policies of the state mean that all individual activities are subject to state approval.

In practice, says Oakeshott, modern states are never pure versions of one or other type, but a mixture of the two or, as he puts it, 'ambiguous'. There has been a drift now for many years, however, towards the state as a corporate, purpose-driven enterprise. After a generation or two of this drift, it becomes part of everyone's understanding of a state that it should take care of things. When the state takes care of things, one by one we lose our freedoms.

Even if we were prepared to accept the loss of civil freedom we might still ask: 'Are modern corporate states any better at delivering on these promises than the fascists and communists were?' And after fifty years of experiment we might say, 'No.'[2] Prosperity has increased as technology brings new ways of exploiting the world — in spite of the fact that corporate governments now cream off roughly fifty percent of national product. As for social justice, inequality in wealth has never been greater and corruption on a huge scale is a fact of life in the corporations and state apparatuses of Europe and America.

It seems the modern corporate democratic state is inefficient, devious and disappointing — just as the totalitarian states were. But could politics be a respectable business, and the state an asset, if both were limited to certain well-defined activities? Such a state of affairs may seem like an impossible dream, romantic nostalgia for a state that never existed. The kind of liberal utopia we might hope to visit on holiday, fleeing from our purpose-driven societies.

Central to the pluralistic ideal of liberal society is the notion of the independent, self-regulating professional. Such freedom and independence is abhorrent to the managers of the enterprise state, who aim to bring all within the fold. The encroach-

---

[2] This was certainly the conclusion of the advocates of economic liberalization during the 1980s.

ments upon the independence of the professions is continual and slow, with appeals to the majority to justify tyrannizing each minority. The teachers need telling what to teach; the doctors need telling how to manage their practices; hospitals need to be run by 'people's representatives'; lawyers make too much money and should be monitored; artists need state sponsorship for their own good. Soon all professionals exist in semi-slavery to 'representatives of the people' as if professionals are not 'people' themselves. Meanwhile the government becomes itself a large corporation expecting obedience, loyalty, servility while giving in return a share of the wealth it has managed to commandeer. Thus a kind of moral slavery manages to establish itself across the professional classes. The implications of this will be explored in detail in the next chapter.

The state-with-a-purpose negotiates its purposes with the electorate. The 'common purposes' won't be shared by all, but they will be supported by enough voters to elect a government. This leads to the familiar 'tyranny by the majority', for the goals will be approved by some but actually detested by others. An extreme example of this today is American foreign policy, which a substantial moral minority has abhorred over many decades.

The pseudo-imperial state

Most of what has been said in this chapter focuses on European political experience, but there is one aspect of the corporate state which Europe has largely left behind. It is this aspect that is the driving force behind American activity in the world today, and that is old-fashioned nationalism.

It might be said that Europe has had its fill of empire. After two devastating world wars, various attempts at genocide including the Holocaust, and a sense that European civilization died somewhere along the way, the appetite for ramming our superiority down others' throats is dead.

America, however, is different. A conviction that the American way should be imposed on the rest of the world is alive and well. But American preeminence is prevented from becoming a true empire in that, for a variety of reasons, America shows no desire to extend the rule of its law to the territories where it gains advantage.

In 1997 an interesting book was published by Yale University Press called *Reconstructing America*. In it an academic attempts to 'take America back' from all the critics who have defamed it. Insults hurled by intellectual crackpots from Europe and from within America are recorded in great detail. The overall impression the book likes to give is of bitter, envious and impotent midgets hurling insults at a dynamic and creative civilization (America) which by its vigour, strength and honesty has come to dominate us all.

Also recorded in detail are defences of America put up by writers of repute. However, criticisms by writers of repute are not quoted at all. George Washington, Mark Twain, Alexis de Tocqueville, Lord Acton and Jacob Burckhardt for instance are either ignored or quoted only in the defence. The book makes interesting reading as an example of how an educated mind provides its own self-censorship. It is an insight into how the ruling interests of America maintain for themselves the fiction that America is a land of freedom and democracy and a force for good in the world.

Part of America's vision of its own superiority is a conviction that other cultures and nations are enmired in one or many varieties of primitive condition. Poverty, ignorance, superstition, hysteria, envy, powerlessness, getting one's hands dirty while growing food — these are all signs of un-American primitivism. For the emancipated, culture itself is primitive when it is not a pick-and-choose affair, but a way of life. The sophisticated American who wears an African bracelet as an ornament views with condescension the tribesman who wears it as a mark of cultural identity.

This kind of national arrogance has not been uncommon among builders of empires. But it has usually led imperialists to impose an element of their own justice on what goes on, if only to temper the exploitative acts of some of its worse conquistadorial elements. In the United States, the *conquistadores* are in charge. The highest legal offices are in the gift of politicians and the law is flexible, depending upon how rich you are. America has blocked attempts at developing international law, except where it regulates trade in favour of corporations. In America's ability to change its ruling class will be the seeds of any future greatness. The great tragedy of America is that its government so often represents the worst of its people.

CHAPTER 4

Serving the Corporate State

Whereas corporations enjoy limited liability, corporate governments appear to enjoy almost zero liability. They can ruin or impair lives with virtually no comeback — just a spell in opposition.

When a government corrupts education, its victims are teachers, whole generations of children, the adults those children become, and finally the self-understanding of an entire civilization. When it mismanages health it damages the lives of doctors, nurses and patients. When it mismanages transport it drives us to distraction; and so on and so on. These offences can turn the details of our lives — where most of us spend most of our time — into little pockets of hell and civilization into a type of advanced slavery.

State activity in any area, funded by taxation, makes it hard for private or self-organizing services to compete. Subsidy gives a commercial advantage to whatever it promotes. When taxpayers have to pay once for services through taxation, they must see quite inordinate advantages in a private version to pay for it again. Thus state intrusion drives out private activity.

Of course there are ideological justifications for state intrusion. A lust for power is not the stated motive. Enforced equality in the name of social justice is the justification for state medicine and education. For state-run transport, there is the practical argument that monopolies should not be handed to private business. For state involvement in the arts, the justification is that 'culture' is an important minority activity which would not flourish without state assistance.

The result in each case is takeover by state 'management specialists'. Gone are organizations that had to compete by being good. The new 'management specialists' have accountability to above, to the latest political ideology imposed and monitored by the state apparatus. And the remit is always to go for appearances, for the short-term benefit of the politicians who employ them, so they can say 'Look how well we are doing!' regardless of results. To keep up appearances (all the old techniques are used, massaging statistics, misrepresenting feedback, putting on a special show for inspectors etc.) employees are required to be part of 'one vast frictionless engine of deceit'.

This is about as far from democracy as you can get. Bogus 'focus groups', which the state sets up to give an illusion of democratic process, are a much-reported mockery. True democracy — that is, where we can all truly hope to have our little bit of influence in what goes on — is served much better in the self-organizing endeavours of people working to provide a service, politics nowhere to be seen. The 'politicization of everything' is also the degradation of everything. The illusion of popular power hands real power to petty and ineffectual tyrants.

Decades of poor delivery have no effect, apparently, on the general belief that politicians one day might, or at least should, 'deliver'. Nor is any recognition paid to the fact that non-delivery is the least of the evils which result when the state takes over. Loss of freedom and integrity right across society might be seen as a greater evil. The loss of civilization itself, when its main constituents are put to use by the state, might be something still more to lament.

Education put to use

Education can be corrupted into promoting all kinds of propaganda — for instance encouraging aggressive nationalism in America and the Arab countries, or propagating twisted versions of history in the segregated schools of Northern Ireland.

In Europe generally such crude propaganda is no longer the issue; the corruption of education is in its being put to use.

The enjoyment of our human inheritance, the quest for self-understanding, the wider adventures in human understanding which have been the breath of life to civilization for a thousand years are set aside; and the lungs of our civilization, the schools and universities, are replaced by socialization industries turning out useful human units. Teachers and pupils may live in despair at this process; but they are impotent in the face of the rational argument that what we want is not a liberal education but a bigger national pie.

Prussia led the way in the provision of state education during the eighteenth century, and in Prussia the political motivation was openly stated — to provide the state with a useful and well-behaved secular citizenry who would be an economic asset to society, domestically peaceful, yet militarily enthusiastic. The state was in no doubt of the power to mould minds which control of education offered. Future citizens — the future workforce of the country — were in their hands.

In Britain, before the Education Act of 1870, there were thousands of small schools organized by churches and workers' self-help groups. These schools were busily supplying education to poor children, most of whom emerged at the very least literate. The vast majority of these schools withered when the state, appropriating money through taxation, supplied 'free' (i.e. compulsorily funded) education. Poor parents, who had to pay for education once through taxes, could hardly afford to pay for it again, so they deserted existing schools and sent their children to state schools instead. From the 1880s on, the private sector became a haven for people able and willing for whatever reason to pay twice.

According to E.G. West, 'It was associations of teachers who were the main advocates of the collectivization of education. The policy was not spontaneously demanded by the people; it had to be sold to them.' An 1861 survey by the Newcastle Commission reported that the idea of free education seemed to most parents insultingly patronizing. 'The sentiment of independence is strong, and it is wounded by the offer of an absolutely gratuitous education.' Compulsory 'free' education as a state monopoly was pushed through by teachers and political ideologues, one commonly stated motive being to reduce the influence of religion in education. Political homogenization was the goal, so 'common values' would be promoted.

State control of the curriculum has increased dramatically since 1976, when Prime Minister James Callaghan declared it was a 'secret garden' which must be opened up to inspection. The curriculum is now set by state-employed experts and, as might be expected, an insane degree of incompetence has been added to a mix of ideological bullying and monopolistic homogeneity. Curricula which are simply impossible to teach are being introduced and teachers are leaving their once-beloved profession in droves.

The 'useful' concept of education has now been imposed by law on the private sector too, and is being introduced to the universities via compulsory research requirements. Replacing the study of poetry with jingle-writing for advertising on university English courses is an example of 'useful' education in action.

State monopoly in education, with the emphasis on passing exams to get jobs, means that children who do not achieve in exams leave school feeling useless; in fact their whole school experience can be one of being made to feel useless. Their resentment and boredom causes problems for others too, as they vent their frustration inside the classroom and out. At the other end of the scale, pupils who might benefit from a liberal education are being processed as corporate cogs, never discovering they had an inheritance to wonder at, delight in — and, from it, to learn what it can mean to be human. No wonder self-obliteration is the main occupation of so many between the ages of eleven and twenty-five.

A university professor said to me recently: 'I am kept so busy describing and justifying what I do to control-freak *apparatchiks*, and churning out unread and irrelevant pseudo-research to meet publication targets, that I have no time to think, to teach, or be a help to my pupils. As for the students, when we do have access to them, we must flatter, we must deceive, we must talk nonsense; the one thing we must never do is educate.'

The idea of liberal education is becoming something of a remote dream, or recollection. When students of the future wish to find out what liberal concept of education fuelled the efforts of their ancestors, will they be able to find texts describing it? Or will books containing such texts have been phased out, joining the millions of books weeded out and dumped every year to make way for the new state-inspired tracts which every up-to-date library must contain? How many libraries even today still contain a definition of a liberal education such as this:

> This, then is what we are concerned with: adventures in human self-understanding. Not the bare protestation that a human being is a self-conscious, reflective intelligence and that he does not live by bread alone, but the actual enquiries, utterances and actions in which human beings have expressed their understanding of the human condition. This is the stuff of what has come to be called a 'liberal' education — liberal because it is liberated from the distracting business of satisfying contingent wants.[1]

or a statement of the importance of its independence, such as this:

> Let any reflecting man think for a moment of the trickery of business, the jobbing of politicians, the slang of newspapers, the vulgarity of fashion, the sensationalism of popular books, the shallowness and cant that dishonour pulpit and defile worship, and he may reasonably rejoice that there is one community which, for a considerable period, takes in its keeping many of the most susceptible and promising of our youth to impart to them better tastes, higher aims, and, above all, to teach them to despise all sorts of intellectual and moral shams.'[2]

Art put to use

Contemporary art sponsored by the corporate state is a recent development. Whereas totalitarian states seize control of art immediately, recognizing its potential to stimulate the imagi-

---

[1]   Oakeshott, 'A Place of Learning.'

[2]   Noah Porter, Inaugural Address at Yale University, 1871.

nation to another way of living, the corporate state has crept up on its victim slowly. State takeover of the arts was enthusiastically welcomed by some artists who hoped to benefit from it, or who were genuine believers in the state as a benefactor.

In corporate Britain, the situation three or four decades on is astonishing. Good contemporary art has been all but extinguished in the state's patronage, replaced with bizarre events mostly involving nothing more than petty bits of nastiness. The techniques of art are no longer taught in most state-sponsored colleges of art. Art from past ages is venerated but its significance has been revised as context-specific, i.e. it speaks to us not with a voice 'relevant' to us today, but as a socio-economic reflection of its age, a justification of whatever ruling interest it served. What a parcel of rogues they are, who thus deceive!

Managing the industry has created a new culture of arts controllers. These *apparatchiks* tend to 'dumb down' relentlessly, way below the point of public demand. The cultural life of these controllers gains a drift of its own, just as any state *apparat* must, and being a member of the 'great and good' demands a continual recognition of profundity in squalid self-hatred; sperm-stained beds, paintings done in shit, corpses, blood, flies and so on. The enterprise of state control, with its selective patronage regardless of any actual public interest, is corrupt from the beginning. Furthermore, large amounts of corporate money follow state funds in a low-risk, high-profit speculative enterprise, turning the art world into a hotbed of incestuous interests.

Fascist state-art celebrated death on the one hand and natural glowing healthy citizens on the other in a way that fitted the cracked psychology of fascism. Soviet art idealized collectivized workers and mechanized production — propaganda for the official ideology. But how does contemporary state art fit with the corporate state? The rationale of a corporate state is that we all need a big state to look after us and monitor what we get up to. Is that why it promotes expressions of life as tedious, disgusting, meaningless, and of humanity as dreary and unredeemable? Certainly such a credo justifies us all needing to be watched over.

There is, however, one way that art in a corporate state fits in with the totalitarian tradition, and that is where it embodies and commercializes the transgressive. It is an act of genius on behalf of the modern corporate world — by which I mean the interplay of corporations and the corporate state — that it has learnt not to suppress, but to commercialize what rebels against itself. Young people out of sympathy or even in a state of hatred with the contemporary world are exploited by that same world as an almost boundless source of spending. The contemporary music business is of course the main example of this, but state contemporary visual art apes the themes of alienation and disgust, to give an illusion of being 'relevant' while creating a convenient speculative commodity.

The head of the chief organ of state art in Britain gave an address recently outlining his credo, and he summed it up by saying the essence of art is transgression. This is a direct inheritance from the Nazi era, when man's duty was to outgrow or transcend his moral self, substituting the cult of transgression for the condition of freedom. Since there is so little freedom in a corporate state, there is little to genuinely admire — the expression of some extraordinary skill perhaps, such as in sports. Outside of this there is the cult of celebrity, where ordinariness mixed with extraordinary ambition and a willingness to do something outrageous is enough to make someone into a vehicle for vicarious living.

Charity put to use

Gifts of charity from the public are usually made without strings attached, and with genuine generosity and good intent (though the outcome may be different from what they intended). But 'aid' made by governments is another matter altogether. It may be tied to arms deals, or purchase of the donor's goods. It may be in support of some great project which will be destructive of many homes and many lives, as in agricultural projects which turn nomadic lands into luxury-food farms run by multinational agribusiness.[3] On many occasions, the money lent has been stolen and re-invested in the donor country by corrupt members of the government to whom it is given; thus the donor country gets the money back immediately and interest payments must be paid by the desperately poor inhabitants of the country who have been 'aided'.

Domestic charity fares not much better, as can be seen in the gradual growth of homeless and wretched, crazy people living destitute on the streets since the state took over our human duties of charity.

Science put to use

The idea of the corporate state received its first manifesto in the writings of Francis Bacon, who was also the first to argue that the only genuine understanding is scientific understanding. Since Bacon no advocate of the corporate state ever ignored the potential of science to help him further his ends. Fascists, communists and third-wayists are alike attracted by its power and the certainty of its ideas. Like Glendower calling up spirits from the vasty deep, they summon science to their aid and, unlike the spirits, science is ready and willing to come.

Science deals in stable and communicable measurements, and in theories about the natural world which inspire the scientists to make those measurements. Theories are tested via experiments designed to exclude all factors save one and the conclusion — theory right or wrong — is a simple one. Furthermore, the conclusion can be confirmed or dismissed by the community of scientists specializing in the same area, who can repeat the experiment and make their own measurements.

This all leads to two quite different but deeply attractive developments. First, science is a world of relative certainty compared to all the other worlds we have to inhabit. Secondly,

---

[3]   I asked the man in charge of one such project, what would happen to those displaced? 'Oh they will sell their sisters as whores and enjoy a much better standard of living.' His wife laughed; 'Or they can all become basketball players in New York!'

practical applications of scientific knowledge give us ever-increasing and multiplying powers over nature.

Planners and policy-makers love simple certainties as well as power. They favour approaches to knowledge that are 'scientific' and thereby more useful. 'Scientific' practitioners of disciplines such as sociology, psychology, and economics pick up government funding and become the favoured group. Hence Nadezhda Mandelstam's complaint that the modern age has to cope not only with the sciences, but the pseudo-sciences as well.

Science has changed utterly since the eager curiosity and organizing passions of its first investigators revealed a whole new way of understanding the world. Science as a way of knowing the world has become insignificant beside science as technique, which offers undreamed-of benefits at unheard-of (and unmeasurable) costs to our future. In the process the tradition of science — to be faithful to measurable, communicable facts and to theorize only within the boundaries of those facts — has been corrupted. The wonderful and playful world which Newton described has receded into the shadows; and Newton knew the place science should occupy in our world when he said:

> I do not know what I may appear to the world but to myself I seem to have been like a boy, playing on the seashore, and diverting myself in now and then finding a smoother pebble or a prettier shell than ordinary, while the great ocean of truth lay all undiscovered before me.

Now, over ninety percent of physicists are employed directly or indirectly by the military, perfecting the arts of death. How has science changed, in service to the corporate state!

Biology is another mine of scientific technique worked by governments and corporations. It is put to use in industrialized medicine, agriculture, and now in the manipulation of our future. Whether the projected cohorts of designer organisms will fare any better than the designer states of the Third Reich or the International Revolution is uncertain. It seems more

likely that some escapee pathogen will bring the foolishness of
the project home to all of us, big time.

Biological science also serves up the usual pseudo-scientific
ideologies for corporate use. Idiotic ideas such as that all
humans are equal in intelligence, or that human intention
should be properly located in 'selfish genes,' hold sway in large
swathes of the corporate-administered community of science.
These ideas are equivalent to fascist racial theories and Soviet
Lysenkoism as crackpot dogma. What they serve is rival
visions of the state: egalitarian socialism in the case of equal
intelligence, a Thatcherite 'selfish economy' in the case of 'selfish genes'. Such pseudo-scientific nonsense would not much
matter, except that in all the noise of factionalism truth is
nowhere to be heard; it offends both sides and is banished.

The scientific community is still further polarized between
corporate employers on the one hand and environmentalist
charities, who have their own axe to grind. The ideology of
environmentalists is that every ill must be blamed on a *lack* of
democracy, and on the corporate West for frustrating democracy where it might otherwise flourish. To observe that democracy drinks willingly from the poisoned chalice of corporate
power is not acceptable. In particular the Third World, now
re-named 'the South', must be regarded as eternally innocent.
Political correctness has made just as thorough a job of muddy-
ing the water as has the corporate state.

'We are apt to think of a civilization as something solid and
external, but at bottom it is a collective dream', Michael
Oakeshott wrote in 1946. 'The project of science, as I understand it, is to solve the mystery, to wake us from our dream, to
destroy the myth; and were this project fully achieved, not only
should we find ourselves awake in a profound darkness, but a
dreadful insomnia would settle upon mankind, not less intol-
erable for being only a nightmare.'

The politicization of everything: factionalism and the corporate state

'The first casualty of war is truth.' Equally, when conversation degenerates into argument, truth goes out for a breather. Arguments are about winning, not establishing truth.[4]

The factionalism of right and left which plagued Europe in the last century was a struggle to determine who should exercise power. Their noisy argument drove out the quieter voices of others who were saying, 'maybe the exercise of power is inappropriate in certain areas'. Meanwhile right and left got on with exercising power where and when they could. Eventually, they became reconciled in the corporate state and now they exercise power simultaneously, right and left arms of the same big thug.

Left and right survive in America too, as attitudes to social problems and to what Big Government should be about. Renamed liberal and conservative, one favours big government as social engineer; the other favours strong, aggressive executive measures at home and abroad. Political correctness tyrannizes the left; the right embraces tyranny of almost any aggressive sort, having expelled the libertarians from among themselves long ago during the Cold War.

The combined operation of left and right in America is clearest in the urban racial minority ghettoes, whose communities have been transformed from underprivileged but fairly peaceful communities into havens of drugs and murder. Denied the rule of law by the machinations of political correctness, fuelled at survival level by welfare, fed drugs and guns by enthusiasts of free enterprise and (allegedly) a collusion between mafia,

---

[4] Plato drew a similar distinction between the 'dialectical' and 'eristic' path to truth. Plato calls an eristic discussion one in which each party tries to prove that he was right and the other wrong. In a dialectical discussion you aim at showing that your own view is one with which your opponent really agrees, even if at one time he denied it; or conversely that it was yourself and not your opponent who began by denying a view with which you really agree. The essence of dialectical discussion is to discuss in the hope of finding that both parties to the discussion are right and that this discovery puts an end to the debate. The philosopher and historian R.G. Collingwood concluded that parliamentary government in Britain ceased to be dialectical after the Second Reform Act.

FBI and CIA, ghettoes have become locations of containment and self-extermination for much of the black population.

Black America could hardly be expected to sign up to corporate serfdom with the same simple shrug as the white community, having only just escaped true slavery. But its being typecast as a nation of irredeemable transgressives, in particular by the popular music industry, is for the most part a commercial expression of white racism. By far the biggest buyers of 'gangsta rap' are white teenage girls trying to enrage their fathers — a kind of racist double-act.

On the international scene, liberal and conservative interests are in tacit agreement on one thing; American interference abroad is a good thing. Liberals want to rid the world of injustice; conservatives want American preeminence on the world stage. The result: for some time to come, there will be no peace, as we shall see in the next chapter.

CHAPTER 5

Plundering the
Nations

'The state founded on sheer crime is compelled in the course of
time to develop a kind of justice and morality, since those of its
citizens who are just and moral gradually get the upper hand',
wrote Jacob Burckhardt in the late 1860's. We can see this principle now at work in Russia, and in varying degrees it has been
at work in many nations including ex-communist and fascist
regimes. But where outsiders finance or provide weapons for
endless strife and insurgence within a state, even the mainte-
nance of rudimentary order becomes an ongoing impossibility.

The principal providers of such destabilizing influences over
the last half-century have been the Soviet Union, the United
States, and more recently pan-Arab Muslim fundamentalists. It
has been a game for almost anyone to play, but these three
groups have been the most active.

The activities of the CIA in this area are described in the following paragraph from an academic, largely pro-CIA perspective:

> The principles behind American democracy, in addition to its dis-
> tinctive political processes, have influenced the nature and effec-
> tiveness of the CIA's work. American democracy came of age
> when the revolt by the indigenous white population of the colo-
> nies produced a virulent and successful sense of nationhood. Ever
> since, this experience has been the bedrock of American anti-impe-
> rialism, and 'nation-building' became one of the CIA's leading
> activities after its formation in 1947. As a result of both the voters'
> rejection of domestic socialist parties and of the totalitarian nature

of the Soviet socialist state, however, the majority of Americans has come to believe that socialism is almost by definition the negation of democracy, and that no truly indigenous and democratic political movement will opt for left-wing politics. In its foreign covert operations, therefore, the CIA has sometimes had to play, not its trump card — encouragement of local nationalism and pride — but its vulnerable card — opposition to a popular local socialist movement.[1]

This describes the political starting-block from which the CIA has financed thugs, murderers, torturers, gangsters, drug-runners, and other kinds of human horror in order to prevent emerging nations choosing socialism. Whole nations have been, and are, the victims of these crimes. In particular, individuals who might help their nations towards a great and independent future are eliminated. If Britain had responded to American moves towards independence in the same way, it would have financed assassins to torture and kill the Sons of Liberty, then financed and armed a junta of the same assassins which would have kept the population in check by torture, murder, and rape.

Nevertheless, the CIA has acted responsibly in the context of American democracy, in the sense that it has pursued accepted public goals within the moral framework laid out for it by the presidential executive to whom it is primarily responsible under the constitution. The extraordinary disparity between what America thinks it is about, and what it is actually about, is nowhere more glaringly apparent than here.

In fact it would appear, from the efforts of a new generation of revisionist historians, that the Jekyll-and-Hyde nature of American democracy was present right from the start. The War of Independence was conducted to the theme tune of life, liberty etc., but under the rhetoric were motives less openly stated: trading aspirations, a resentment of British insistence that the colonists should respect native American land rights, and a commitment to slavery — which was not supported in English law.

In the War of 1812 a large number of slaves had followed away the British troops. The Treaty of Ghent that closed the War of 1812 pro-

---

[1]   *The CIA and American Democracy*, R. Jeffreys-Jones, 1989 p.4.

vided for an arbitration of this matter. Slavery being involved, the government followed up this matter with almost religious enthusiasm. After many years England paid $1,204,960, rather than return black men, who had once breathed English air, and were therefore free, to slavery in the 'land of the free'.[2]

In practice, liberal democracy is about the one form of government America does not actively support, if only for the good reason that where it exists it does not need external support. It may need military protection, and this America has provided, especially when the enemy is also its own as in Western Europe during the Cold War. But where America is involved in the covert supply of arms, finance and intelligence, its client regimes are about as far from 'liberal' or 'democratic' as it is possible to be.

Even if the US *were* promoting 'liberal democracy' would not this be an imposition. Is it necessarily the best and most practical form of government for young nations, with perhaps a large proportion of uneducated voters, a history of colonial rule, oddly-drawn boundaries and conflicting tribal loyalties? Does it not in any case produce a strange kind of post-civilizational nightmare where it holds sway in the West?

As an example of democracy having a deleterious effect upon a nation we may take recent events in Venezuela. In the 1970s, Venezuela was effectively ruled by an oligarchy presiding over a reasonably stable and prosperous society, though as usual there were injustices afflicting large swathes of the population. But not only was the oil industry domestically owned, large sections of the American oil industry were in Venezuelan ownership too.

Now, after a few decades of populist democracy, the country has ground to a standstill. Presidents were elected to power on promises of land reform and nationalization. The nationalized oil industry has seized up and the rest of the country's assets have fled abroad — mostly to Florida — along with the oligarchy who used to run the country. Land, vulnerable to seizure by *campesinos*, has become almost valueless. Anarchy-by-

---

[2]   From John Maxcy Zane, *The Story of Law.*

democracy has taken over. The wealth of Venezuela now resides, along with most rich Venezuelans, in America.

Another kind of degradation may occur when a traditional monarchical government breaks down with the introduction of democracy. Imagine a kingdom insulated from the modern world — a mountain kingdom perhaps, that the tourists have missed. Imagine it peaceful; by some happy chance it is well-governed by its monarch and a council of elders. Agriculture by time-honoured methods sustains its populace, and simple laws preserve peace and tranquility.

In order not to idealize beyond all possibility this mountain kingdom, let us imagine its population kept stable by some methods unpalatable to Western tastes. Political innovators are not paid much attention; cultural developments take place fairly slowly; some diseases remain unchecked by medicines common in the West; and immigration in large numbers is not welcomed.

As far as the global markets are concerned, our mountain kingdom is an irrelevance: there is traffic neither to nor from it. But wait! To the enterprising global marketeer it is not an irrelevance but a wasted opportunity. There is a great deal of money to be made in offering it the advantages of Western civilization!

According to Vandana Shiva, plastic packaging is the Trojan horse which facilitates the arrival of all the other delights of Western 'civilization'. For reasons of hygiene, packaging is made compulsory — with the help of a small donation to someone influential in the legislature. Landfill sites will be the first requirement of our kingdom transformed; and heavy machinery to shift the earth. Next will come weapons systems, airports, tourism and debt. The old king has to go because he cannot be bribed. One of his more ruthless courtiers forms a political party, which sweeps the board when foreign funding is cunningly distributed to the right people.

Next, an agrarian revolution hands land ownership over to foreign corporations. Efficient modern methods result in the production of lucrative, foreign-exchange-earning luxury goods for Western markets. This foreign exchange is badly needed, because the national debt is growing. Meanwhile medical specialists are ensuring that the population multiplies exponentially and, its land taken over for more efficient use, the multiplied population is piling up in shanty towns where refuse, violence, prostitution and open sewers have replaced countryside, tranquility, courtships and clean-flowing rivers.

The shanty towns are alive with the sound of televisions, broadcasting fantasies of escape from the hell of enforced uselessness. Drugs will proliferate for the same end. The West has arrived in all its glory, and money is flowing all over the place in large quantities.

Such mountain communities barely still exist; Nepal went a way similar to the one described above. Bhutan, under intense pressure with armed refugees from neighbouring conflicts, is probably the last tiny kingdom on earth still defending itself against the modern world. A hundred and fifty years ago, it was not just tiny kingdoms that were undergoing Westernisation. When the US knocked on the door of feudal Japan in 1854, Japan was just such a wasted opportunity. It had kept out foreigners for over two hundred years. The Americans, suspicious that Dutch and English traders were getting trade concessions when they weren't, sent in gunboats to open up Japan to the modern world. The rest, as they say, is history.

Economics and globalization

In practice, the kinds of state America likes to promote are 'ones we can do business with.' Corrupt oligarchies are easier than democracies for American business. Their governments are easily influenced; the wealth stays in the hands of a few who re-invest it in America, and debts made to the wealthy pile up on the poor, who have to pay interest on them back to the West.

As for the corporations, they act in a climate of almost non-existent international law, and the payments they make are to all intents and purposes untraceable. Those payments fund, directly or indirectly, activities like the roaming armies trying to corner the trade in valuable minerals such as 'coltan', the columbite/tantalite mineral used in mobile phone manufacture.These activities destabilise countries such as the Congo which are unlucky enough to be rich in what the West desires.

The language of economics has changed greatly since Adam Smith. He combined psychological and sociological insights to make the key propositions of an essentially moral argument, which he then supported with historical examples. This is a typical sentence from *The Wealth of Nations*:

> Country gentlemen and farmers, dispersed in different parts of the country, cannot so easily combine as merchants and manufacturers, who being collected into towns, and accustomed to that exclusive corporation spirit which prevails in them, naturally endeavour to obtain against all their countrymen the same exclusive privilege which they generally possess against the inhabitants of their respective towns.

By way of contrast, this is a typical passage from a modern economic journal, taken off the internet:

> According to loanable funds theory, a rise in thrift directly and immediately lowers the rate of interest unless obstructed by either one of two specific interfering factors, namely, a simultaneous rise in hoarding or by credit contraction. Different versions of loanable funds theory were proposed and a considerable variety of specific models put forward, but the essence of loanable funds theory may be suitable expressed in terms of the following simple loanabe funds market equation:
>
> $$S + \Delta M - H = I$$
>
> with S and I standing for net national saving and net national investment over some period of time, and ΔM and H for changes in the stock of money and net hoarding respectively and over the same period of time.

The effort to become a science has deprived economics of its ability to look at the whole picture, to understand its place in the scheme of human affairs. The paragraph just quoted concerns the effects of money movements *within* an economic system, not the mutual interactions of economic systems and our wider lives. In a science, everything must be measurable or it means nothing; but the most important things in life are not stable communicable measurements. Relationships with friends and family, with work, with nature or the city streets; choices made for 'irrational' reasons, the things one loves; the sense of past, present and future; one's pleasure at a sunset or the singing of birds: none of these can become stable, communicable measurements, so none are to be found in the world of science (though obviously it is possible for scientists to enjoy them too).

In becoming a science, economics has — like most other sciences — become a source-book of techniques. These techniques are pursued, logically enough, in the interests of those who employ the economists. If we would consider the effects of these techniques on the wider welfare or future prospects of humanity, we must look beyond 'scientific economics' to more general human observations about money, wealth and the world we all inhabit.

The first puzzle about American wealth is: Where does it all come from? They don't manufacture a lot any more and many homes in Europe probably don't have a single item made in America. The odd few bits and pieces with an American label were probably made in the Far East and 'sourced' by American companies.[3] The only time you are likely to be the recipient of a piece of genuine American manufacture is if you're shot or bombed, or step on a land-mine.

America is still a huge exporter of grain for bread and animal food, which is why it is annoyed when foreign markets try to resist its genetically engineered crops. It also exports machinery and machine tools, and computers when it can compete. Over a third of its 'export' income consists of payments on intellectual property rights — on items such as software, entertainment and medicines — of which more later. It exports raw material in huge quantities — cotton, coal and timber. But none of these account for the huge disparity between American wealth and the rest of the world. This disparity shows up a little in the ever-growing debt mountain, which in some magic way America manages to cope with. The prospect of this magic coming to an end must be enough to haunt the dreams of any American who contemplates it.

The debt mountain currently stands at nearly seven trillion dollars. This kind of figure is hard to get a grasp of, but a little

[3] 'Manufacturing is now all about market access,' as one business handbook puts it.

elementary maths can help. Supposing one million dollars in hundred dollar bills stands eighteen inches high — lower than the average kitchen chair — then a billion would stand as high as the Empire State building. A trillion is a thousand Empire-State-building-high piles; seven trillion is obviously seven thousand of these piles. And a million is still below the height of a kitchen chair.

It might be a matter of wonder that America manages to pay the interest on all this debt. Much of the debt is to its own wealthy citizens via the federal bank, so the interest is paid out of taxes on those who work, and paid to the rich; a kind of inverted Robin Hood scenario. Some has to be paid to the foreign investors who have dutifully bailed America out, which is one reason for the unpopularity of the Japanese. But in other cases it would seem that America gets away with paying no interest at all, and even gets away with the schoolboy's dream of making money by printing it; for the trillions outlined below do not even count as part of the national debt.

Monopoly money

Being the monopoly provider of the world's principal currency seems to be a large unmeasured factor in American wealth. The uncovering of billions of dollars of cash in Iraq illustrated a scam which runs like this. America buys oil; the cash in dollars goes to a corrupt dictator who stores it 'on behalf of his people'. The dollars sit unspent in huge piles, demanding no interest off anyone, and not being used for any purchase against American assets. So America has got the oil — as long as those dollars sit unused — for the price of printing the bills. (This might seem to be a reason why America should not have invaded Iraq until one considers that in 2002 Saddam Hussein changed the currency he demanded for 'his' oil from dollars to euros. Did he have intentions of redeeming all those stashed dollars? Could Bush afford *not* to be mad, especially as the idea was catching on — Syria and North Korea were following Iraq's example.) How much money is sitting around the world in similar storehouses in other corrupt regimes is anyone's guess. In this way, corrupt regimes seem to work in America's favour.

A second, related bit of good luck for the US is the number of unstable countries in the world whose own currencies are so dodgy that US dollars are the currency for any serious cash transaction. Again, America has purchased assets with these dollars, which then go into circulation in the foreign country demanding neither interest nor repayment until the country returns to stability. In this way at least, unstable economies seem to be a hidden US asset.

Another bit of good luck for American wealth is the illegal drugs trade. Conducted mostly in high-denomination dollar bills, this trade is the third largest in the world after arms and oil. Again, these trillions running round the world represent interest-free loans until they are redeemed; which will be never, as long as the illegal drug trade is there and needs them. Indeed, as the drugs trade gets bigger and bigger, more and more dollars are needed. This scam carries the added attraction that every now and then a large amount of currency can be confiscated and re-possessed.

George Bush Snr. is credited with the remark, 'The American lifestyle is not negotiable.' Did he mean that any restraint on the scams listed above is not negotiable? Perhaps the Iraq war is a practical indication of his meaning. Without such wars, it is a mystery how the American lifestyle will continue.

Robber banks

'Don't rob a bank, join one! Then you can rob whole countries!'

A merchant banker was explaining to me the pecking order among banks. Top of the heap apparently are bulge-bracket investment banks, robber banks *extraordinaires*.

'Those are the bastards I'm really envious of,' he said. 'They take on whole countries and strip them down.'

'What do you mean?' I asked him.

'Well, imagine a communist country which is emerging from five decades of state ownership and privatizing everything — toll roads, communications, water, power. The communists don't know how to go about this, but as individuals they're greedy bastards like everyone else. So, someone smart from the bank approaches the head honcho — say the party boss for the province — and says, "We'll arrange the sell-off. We'll help arrange a nice big investment in your benefit and — here's the rub — the whole caboodle will double in value the day after privatization, because we're going to price it nice and low. When all's said and done, you'll have maybe a hundred million of your own stashed in the bank! Meanwhile, our responsibility is to underwrite it, so we'll invest a hundred million of our own too; oh yes, and of course we know lots of investors who will be glad to take on the rest!"'

'So you mean,' I said, 'what was an asset owned by, say, the Chinese or Hungarian people becomes overnight an asset owned by foreigners, who've effectively picked it up for free?'

'Half-owned, dummy!' he replied. 'The other half — or maybe 51% — goes to the provincial government, who of course are often just a teeny bit dodgy themselves. You ever noticed how many big dudes in those countries started life as provincial governors?'

'But doesn't that have a huge effect on a country — when half its assets are suddenly owned by someone else?'

'Are you trying to make me cry?' he said.

'Does anyone object to this?'

'Who is there to object?' he replied. 'People who would object probably don't know what's going on. Oh — and remember the word 'greenshoe'. Banks can make you rich overnight if they so wish. They hold back chunks of these IPO's for grace-and-favour distribution; it's like picking and choosing who they hand out free money to. That's their biggest power of all.'

Intellectual property rights

Intellectual property rights are rights established in law enabling a creator or inventor to exclusively profit from his or her 'intellectual property' for a number of years. The justification for this privilege is that it encourages creativity and invention by providing a possibility of reward, and creativity and invention are a benefit to us all. The whole area is notoriously difficult to get right from the legislator's point of view. How can it give enough away to encourage innovation, without creating a system open to abuse?

Intellectual property rights in law effectively create a monopoly of some type or other, which is why they need special justification to be acceptable. Most people recognize that society benefits all round, from giving a limited monopoly for a limited period of time to the inventor or creator.

So far, so good. But why they are a transferable asset is another matter. Railway tickets, for instance, have clearly written on them: 'This ticket is not transferable.' Why an intellectual property right should be transferable to a corporation is a puzzle; for from then on, only the corporation will benefit, unless the creator has come to an agreement with the corporation. Corporations, as we have seen, are powerful and not noted for generosity except towards themselves. Nor can the inventor stop the corporation 'burying' the invention because it is a competitive threat to some current and lucrative product.

Global agreements on intellectual property rights have been fiercely negotiated by the American government, which has been as keen on pushing developments in international trade agreements as it has been keen on frustrating developments in international law. It has pushed for lengthier time limits on monopolies and ever looser definitions of what might constitute an 'invention'. The reason is not hard to locate: according to Vandana Shiva, more than a third of America's foreign earnings come from intellectual property rights.

The extraordinary power and advantage that corporations gain by being able to own such rights is not in the public interest, for the simple reason that it provides a monopoly on the manufacture of goods, and for a long period of time. Inventors, who must rely upon corporations for access to the markets, are seldom able to negotiate a good return for themselves. The situation is more straightforward, though no less satisfactory, when an inventor is employed by a corporation, for then the corporation owns the invention from the start.

Next comes the question: What qualifies as an invention? For instance, can 'life forms' be inventions? Can traditional medical knowledge be effectively patented for mass production by multinational corporations? The answer to both of these is yes. New 'inventions' include seed that has been tinkered with genetically. Mass production methods for traditional folk medicines have also been patented. Other dodgier bits of business like lab-created viruses targeting a specific pest are also patented for use, even when many scientists protest that it is tantamount to inviting disaster.

With huge amounts of money at stake, the full force of US government and corporate propaganda, including political pressure at high level and payments that corrupt the politics of many nations, is brought to bear to get these products accepted. Wild moral blackmails are also broadcast, like the younger President Bush's assertion that those who resist GM food are in favour of starving Africans. These moral blackmails are in stark contradiction to bona fide research and enrage third world activists with their cynical opportunism.

Intellectual property rights, designed as rewards for creativity and invention, have become tools in the struggle to establish global manufacturing monopolies by multinational corporations. Suggestions have been made that inventors, not corporations, should be solely rewarded; and with royalty payments, not monopoly control. This would prevent the abuse of monopoly production, and also prevent innovations being killed by corporations to prevent competition. But there is no significant democratic interest in the problem — by significant I mean large enough to be noticeable in a majority democracy.

Those who prophesy gloom and doom from these developments do so from familiarity with the lives of farmers and peasants and local economies — from observing the effects already evident of corporate dominance in our lives, from a passionate feeling that if we do not preserve what remains of the world's biodiversity we are handing to our children a tainted and sickened planet and from an awareness that in Nature nothing is ever 'contained'. From this point of view, using the reproducing units of life and disease as if they were cards on a gambling table is profligacy of an order we have not seen before.

The psychology of these addicts to corporate greed showed itself in a conversation I once had with an oilman. He was talking about oil placed by God (who can be a challenging fellow) underneath land occupied by other people.

'There may be monkeys in the trees, roaches in the dirt and sand-niggers on the ground; but God meant oil for those who can make use of it.' (It has to be said, he was drunk at the time.)

'How do you mean?' I said.

'It's our technology. Our civilization. Those guys just happen to be sitting there in their tents on top of where the oil happens to be. Bleeding heart liberals said we should give 'em a whole load of money, and we do! But it doesn't do them any good. We should never have given 'em a nickel. They didn't even know the meaning of property till we taught 'em!'

He rambled on without needing another prompt.

'The fish in the sea belong to those who go out and get 'em out! That's natural enough. Is oil any different? God gave this earth to those who till it with the sweat of their brows.'

'So the oil belongs to...?' I was still not quite clear who his 'we' was; was it white people, was it Americans, was it 'the West'?

'To those who have the savvy and the *cojones* to get it out.'

Suddenly it clicked: his 'we', the group he identified with, his tribe or band of brothers, was the men and women in his organization; the riggers, the geologists, the secretaries, the explosives people, all the people involved in the great corporate enterprise of which he was part. Only his second loyalty was to the larger organization called 'America': the US army which would protect him and the US politics which would maintain his freedom to exploit. His 'America' was not what others might think it to be, it was an organization for the protection of piracy and plunder.

How the founders of America[4] — Washington, Hamilton, Madison, Jefferson — would be spinning in their graves! —

---

[4]   Also John Locke, on account of the corruption of his property theory.

though to Mark Twain my drinking companion would have been no stranger.

After that conversation I understood the mentality of the multinational corporations and what Thomas Jefferson said after serving two terms as president: 'Merchants have no country. The mere spot they stand on does not constitute so strong an attachment as that from which they draw their gains.'

The 'interests of merchants' are of course diverse. For instance, arms manufacturers and cement exporters might welcome war with — for instance — Iraq, whereas Hollywood might be nervous about the effect on sales of its films to Arab countries. By favouring one set of merchants, government is likely to enrage another. So what does it mean, to say that the interests of merchants can predominate in government?

It means that government activities abroad are directed in pursuit of merchants' interests of monopoly and advantage, as against the sovereign interests of stability and mutual prosperity. We see this preference at work in the actions of successive American governments, which squander the goodwill of the world towards America by sponsoring the activities of corporate robbers. And not only America; the governments of Europe and all nations aspiring to Western standards of affluence must join in the competitive race.

So all over the earth power drifts away from indigenous peoples and towards corporations. The world has been given over to grey marauders, politicians and businessmen in suits who put on baseball caps when they want to show they are 'of the people'. Their business is to isolate and seize the wealth of the world. When costs are ugly, they are if possible hidden. Criminality and fraud are only to be deplored when they are perpetrated on the voters and shareholders of the West. The media, fringe groups and various consumer groups are left to operate as our conscience, which they do with gusto, but with limited effect on the democratic consumer society which funds their existence.

CHAPTER 6

Eyeball to Eyeball:
The fight against evil

We wuz eyeball to eyeball and the other guy just blinked. — John Wayne

Like Goya's giants, facing each other in a swamp and battering each other with clubs while they sink, the US and the Islamic Arab nations are an alarming spectacle for the rest of the world. Both civilizations have exhausted their own valued resources — the US its oil, Arabia its land — and both make allegiance to a tyrannizing culture the mainspring of their lives. They differ in that whereas the Arabs long ago gave up their imperialist dreams, the US is insatiably intent upon everyone else's assets — and in Arab lands, that means oil.

America does what it does in the world in the name of freedom and democracy. What democracy means in America has been the subject of another chapter. What freedom means to the ruling class of Americans was the subject of a note jotted down by the historian Acton in 1861 and there is not much to add to it today:

> Their notion of liberty is not = security, nor = self-government, but participation in the government of others; power, not independence; aggression, not safety — that is, always contrary to what it ought to be.

Islam and America are similar in many ways. Both have absorbed people from many different ethnic groups and cultures into a uniting culture. The following description of cultural despotism could fit either Islam or America, though it was made about Islam in the 1860s by Jacob Burckhardt:

> The strongest proof of real, extremely despotic power in Islam is the fact that it has been able to invalidate, in such large measure, the entire history (customs, religion, previous ways of looking at things, earlier imagination) of the peoples converted to it. It accomplished this only by instilling into them a new religious arrogance which was stronger than everything and induced them to be *ashamed* of their past.

The religious arrogance of America is to believe that the American way is good, and that the rest of us need it. Further, while American lives are sacred, other lives are of little consequence. The war with Iraq furnishes dozens of examples, just as did the Vietnam war, of the casual killing of civilians by soldiers: cars sprayed with bullets so an American 'grunt' can 'bust his cherry'; next day a whole family wiped out in nervous reaction to some distant noise; all without any redress for 'liberated' populations.

Americans who find the tyrannizing triviality of their culture a source of shame or worry are marked and shunned as unpatriotic, undemocratic — and now Euro-centric, which is rapidly becoming a mark of Cain.

Islamic and American fundamentalisms share another quality: they are both corruptions of what is good in their traditions. An Arab friend of mine told me of a fierce argument he witnessed between two theologians, one traditional and one fundamentalist. After a pause in the argument, the traditionalist said; 'You know, you are guilty of the worst of heresies: you worship not Allah but Islam.' In other words, not God, but Power. In America too, the fundamentalists worship not freedom or liberty but power.

The faction which currently leads America, fraudulently elected to power on a smaller percentage of the vote than that which brought Hitler to power in Germany, can for the moment afford to ignore criticism. Businessmen will profit from their activities and they are assured of the votes of all those Americans whose identities require the constant refreshment of knowing that they are members of the most powerful nation on earth.

Meanwhile Israel's struggle for existence, already a precarious thing, has been caught up in the struggle. The vast payola donated to Israel by America for acting as its big stick in the Middle East has done its bit to corrupt Israeli democracy and civil life just as it corrupts every nation it touches. The marshalling of so much energy and effort within the state of Israel into a struggle for continued existence has carried with it temptations that have not been avoided; of giving power to those least squeamish about breaking the law, of specifying the franchise so that it excludes the Palestinian minority, and of thereby becoming an institutionally racist state.

Concerning the displacement of Palestinians, it has seemed a singular outrage in our times, but it is far from singular in history; every nation in the world has been formed by waves of conquest and displacement as well as by immigration. Maybe in the future humanity will have an effective international law against such endeavours, but it has not had one up to now. Meanwhile history unfolds its familiar ironies: since the Palestinians replaced the Jews as the principal diaspora of the world, they have also replaced them as the most highly educated people on Earth.

At the same time, the spectre of anti-Semitism returns to Europe as nasty and weak-minded people gather under its banner to blame the whole mess on Israel/the Jews. The idea that 'the Jewish lobby' over and above all other influence groups in American politics is to blame for American foreign policy seems particularly cracked and off-beam when it is a self-styled 'Christian' oil lobby that inhabits the corridors of the White House.

During the Suez crisis, when European powers were making common cause with Israel against Egypt, America objected vociferously and intervened. But American public opinion about Israel — the kind of sentiments expressed in bars, in homes and restaurants — changed radically during the week of the Six Day War. The devastating defeat of the Arab nations by Israel provoked two reactions: an immediate one of admiration for an act of overwhelming and effective violence, and a long-term realization that this violence could be put to use in serving 'American interests'.

As far as American public opinion is concerned, the Jews have one thing to recommend them; they 'kick Arab butt'. America was, and by many accounts still is, a society tainted with anti-Semitism,[1] but that anti-Semitism has been put on hold while Israel holds the key to the pursuit of American interests in the Middle East. The distinctive asset of the Jews which can aid 'American interests' is the military presence and strength of the state of Israel.

Power is the primary appetite of the majority American, who is not so happy commanding people as commanding machines. He judges himself by how much power he has over his environment; his power to do, to buy, to own, to consume, to use, and by using to destroy. This kind of power needs energy to drive it. If Joe America dragged by himself his RV, with his family inside it, from Texas to California it would take more than his life's energy and ingenuity to achieve it; with a few tanks of 'gas' he can do it in speed, comfort and style.

Having squandered his own resources of 'gas' in record time, Joe America needs other people's gas to continue his gluttonous progress. 'The American lifestyle is not negotiable' said the older Bush to applause from the majority. The moral minority feels sick and impotent to change anything. Equally impotent in the large arena are those who live another kind of 'American lifestyle'; the inhabitants of the racial ghettoes, those excluded for whatever reason from pursuit of the American Dream in all its shallow affluence, those who live as best as they can apart from the mainstream.

The growth of federal power and fights against evil

The principal fights against evil during which the United States has increased its federal power at home and abroad have been five: the fight against slavery, the fight against German imperial ambition in the First World War, the fight against Nazism,

---

[1]   Chaim Potok wrote of anti-Semitism in America as 'a polluting white noise, barely heard, barely sensed, but always present'. But he added in this context — 'Those who say America is evil know nothing of Europe.' (*Wanderings*, 1978, p. 522.)

the fight against communism and now the fight against terror. Other lesser ones are: against unemployment (the New Deal), the war on poverty in the 1960s, and the war on drugs over the last thirty years.

Any kind of war requires a marshalling of national assets and may involve curtailments of civil liberties. A common struggle makes claims on patriotic citizens to unite in a consensus, suppressing any reservations they might have about the way the goal is being pursued. After the war is over, there is usually an effort on behalf of the public to reclaim some of the liberties lost, but the effort is usually only partly successful.

Governments are often accused of using strife, even of stirring up trouble, to get their country united behind them. 'Get the people to believe they are under attack, and you can get them to do anything!' said Goebbels. War has rescued many an unpopular politician from oblivion, but it is a risky strategy, as General Galtieri of Argentina found out in 1982 and as Bush and Blair may find out too.

During some of America's fights against evil, the American federal effort has been accused of prolonging the evil it is combating. For instance, the great Southern statesman Calhoun complained that slavery would have been abandoned long before, had the North not used it as a moral weapon in the battle to promote industrialization at the South's expense. Again, during the fight against communism, the two communist countries which survived longest were the two under most consistent American military pressure — Cuba and North Korea. As regards the Soviet Union, the attitude taken by the United States — that only the attrition of competitive military build-up would bring the Cold War to an end — may have prolonged the stranglehold of the communist regime.

In the fight against Islamic fundamentalist terror, the American government is accused not only of prolonging the evil but of instigating it too. Acts of huge massacre are obviously evil; but one can only wonder that it took so long for September 11th 2001 to occur, given the hatred which American activity in the region had been stirring up for decades. American involvement in the Middle East is well-documented and no one disputes the main grievances aired by Islamic fundamentalists.

No one disputes, for instance: that the US props up governments in the region, both illiberal and undemocratic, which torture and murder fundamentalists; that it blocked the democratic election of a fundamentalist government in Algeria; that it aggressively markets products which are offensive to Islam; that it has undermined Iran for many years; that it supports a militant Israel; and that it interferes in many covert ways in the region, first supporting this and then that armed group, so that even now the extent to which the CIA helped Saddam gain power is unclear. A relentless pursuit of power has been disguised as a promotion of freedom.

The following example illustrate the almost routinized mayhem which America stirs up in the Islamic world. In an interview given in 1988, Zbigniew Brzezinski outlined his successful attempt to bring about war between the Soviet Union and Afghanistan when he was National Security Advisor to President Carter. He used the CIA to aid Islamic extremists who were then fighting the socialist government of Afghanistan, and thereby he provoked the Soviet invasion of Afghanistan. This he was proud of, because it gave the Soviet Union

> its Vietnam War. Indeed, for almost ten years Moscow had to carry on a war unsupportable by the government, a conflict that brought about the demoralization and finally the breakup of the Soviet empire.

This is an example of the extraordinary insouciance of the American majority government, instigating the degradation of whole nations, the maiming and butchering of hundreds of thousands of people, on some arcane theory almost no more than a whim. (There is another theory about the fall of the Soviet Union: that communism collapses because the system doesn't work, and because everyone in the end values freedom a little). This example of American behaviour abroad is just one among thousands listed in books like *Rogue State* by William Blum and *Boomerang!* by Mark Zepezauer — books unread by all good Americans.

CHAPTER 7

The Rule of Law

The rule of law bakes no bread, it is unable to distribute loaves or fishes (it has none), and it cannot protect itself against external assault, but it remains the most civilized and least burdensome conception of a state yet to be devised.

With this sentence, Michael Oakeshott outlines the character of law as a means whereby we may live in proximity with each other with as little strife as possible, while remaining free to lead our lives within the conditions it sets.

There is obviously a great deal of difference between a law such as one that forbids murder, and a law which makes all Jews wear yellow patches. The most obvious difference is that one seems sensible and indispensable while the other seems offensive and indefensible. But can we distinguish in a more fundamental way between the two kinds, so we can call one kind authentic and the other a corruption of the very idea of law? Is there a criterion to determine whether a particular law is true to the nature of law?

Oakeshott locates this difference in the principle of impartiality, which means the law must treat all alike; it must not favour one individual or group over another. No person or class should be above the law; neither should a person or class be treated as deserving of special favours.

If a law is made to further a particular purpose, it loses this one essential characteristic. It ceases to be impartial, for no purpose is so 'common' that all citizens will voluntarily subscribe to it. The law becomes an oppressor of some, a favouritiser of others. This is true whether the purpose is thoroughly and obviously obnoxious, as was that of the Nazis, or whether the purpose is to engineer a decent society and improve the national standard of living, as much modern European law-making or 'policy' is designed to do.

In the case of the Nazis, the law was partial in that it gave advantage to vicious thugs. It is worth remembering that of those who designed and set in motion the Holocaust, all but one were lawyers. In the case of modern Europe, where laws are made to promote affluence and social harmony, the law allows or allocates enormous powers to corporations and agencies of state control.

A commentator on South America — I believe it was Richard Feynman, the bongo-playing nuclear physicist — observed that in political discourse there he never heard disapproval of torture *per se*, only disagreement about who should be torturing whom. Similarly, in modern European states including Britain it is assumed that government legislation should have a role in almost everything; only whose side it should be on is open to debate.

When the state is empowered to distribute favours it must take sides and judge between various interest groups, granting this one favours at the expense of that. The scene is set for civil strife. All have to clamour for favours from the state just to stay abreast. The 'politicization of everything' follows. Nothing can flourish on its own without political support; part of everyone's job becomes to consider their position vis-à-vis the state. A monopoly of what-is-approved replaces the diversity of what-people-like.

Is the state a competent and fair distributor of favours, or does power go to its head? History would suggest that the benevolence, let alone the competence, of state power is one of the madder illusions of humanity, particularly after the examples of communist and fascist states. It seems there is an in-built preference, in democratic majorities, to believe in the state as fairy godmother rather than to accept the burdens of freedom.

There are, however, some snags in the simple design of the opposite kind of state, that is the state as a rule of law with no purpose of its own. Unavoidably, the state must take on certain instrumental roles: for instance, very few would deny that the state should undertake a limited redistribution of wealth — this has been regarded as both necessary and just since Solon's day. The state must also commandeer some of our resources for the defence of the nation, given the unavoidable realities of aggression and human nature. And it is recognized that in cases where a monopoly situation is inherently unavoidable, a public service industry is best administered by the state.

Once the necessity of these exceptions is acknowledged, constant public monitoring is needed to make sure they are not abused. Obvious examples of abuse are corrupt defence contracts, inefficient state-run businesses, the rich being taxed vengefully in order to 'make their pips squeak,' or 'defence of the realm' being abused to justify aggressive war.

But supposing the state was effectively confined to these boundaries, what kind of society would we expect to see?

We would expect a society where all are free to carry on endeavours, individually or in groups, without interference from the state. The law would set conditions upon our activities — for instance, you can't murder or rob in order to get what you want. The state would not take on the job of engineering us into good health, good manners, or good citizens; that would be left to the moral climate of the time (there might actually then *be* a moral climate). All things which flourished for centuries outside government control would be left once again to flourish — charity, the arts, education, medicine, science, maybe even the environment. Independent thought might even arise from the ashes of our education system. And competitive business activity would no longer be strangled by monstrous corporations, for the state would not recognize as personae corporations for whom criminal and moral responsibility are close to an irrelevance. It would not sponsor favoured enterprises at all, but leave people free to find and make for themselves what they wanted to sponsor and enjoy. Art and culture might once more become meaningful concepts. Once again, local interests would manage themselves, and national interests would be run by people who know what they are talking about. Democracy would be a living reality, active in all areas of our lives, rather than the once-in-a-while chimera it is today.

Law and morality

Since a civilized society depends upon its citizens behaving morally as well as legally, there is a question as to where morality ends and law begins. Generally, crossing the line from law to morality is to go from an area where the absolute authority of a particular rule — for instance against murder — is easily and generally acknowledged, to an area where rules meet with less general agreement. To make a law against marital infidelity, for instance, or against kosher/halal butchery, is to tyrannize one section of the community with the moral scruples of another.

Definite formulations of morality are notoriously difficult. Even the simplest rule — 'do as you would be done by' — is open to objection. One person might want to be assaulted and beaten for sexual pleasure; that doesn't mean he should go around doing this to others. Morality is practical; its workings will be different in different situations, and formulating it invites contradictions. A case in an American high school illustrates the point. A boy turns up in a T-shirt with words in big letters offensive to women: 'Suck my d__k'. A girl in his class complains he is destroying her guaranteed right to a non-hostile educational environment. The boy says he has a right to freedom of expression. The legal implications are horrendous — the school's legal officer will have a nervous breakdown and lawyers will make millions arguing it through the courts. A situation which any moral human being would have dealt with by enforcing common (moral) courtesy has become a major legal nightmare.

Civilization, not in ideology but in simple history, has been the coming together of different peoples to form complex societies, and civilized law is concerned to let that flourish. The diversity of peoples is not a condition beloved by all, however. A theocracy is an exclusive tyranny by the morality of one particular group which, diversity being endemic to humanity, will be felt as tyranny even by some in the group itself.

The law, as it becomes more complex, is fully workable only at great expense. Lawyers of course benefit from this financially, and become part of the plutocracy. Others in the plutocracy also benefit, as they use procedural technicalities to escape justice. In America it is often observed that legal mechanisms put in place to protect the poor are used by the rich to avoid justice. The poor cannot afford the full process of the law, nor can the state afford to supply it on the poor's behalf. Justice for the poor has to be administered in a spirit of pragmatism, or the system would seize up.

The tendency of laws to proliferate has been complained about for thousands of years. 'As formerly we suffered from crimes, now we suffer from laws', wrote Tacitus (b. AD 56). 'The most desirable laws are those that are rarest, simplest and most general; I even think it would be better to have none at all, than to have them in such numbers as we have', wrote Montaigne (b. 1533). Legislative assemblies like to make laws; that is what they are there for. Zaleucus, supposedly the first Greek ruler (650 BC) to have laws written down, found his assembly making new laws so fast that he invented a device to restrain the enthusiasm of proposers; they should appear in the assembly with a rope around their neck, and if the law was not adopted they should be hanged.

The proliferation of laws, especially when they are instrumental to some purpose, obscures their relation to the preservation of justice as a high ideal demanding all of our acquiescence. De Tocqueville thought that a respect for law was the most significant restraint upon majority democracy in America. Practices which might get a big 'yes' vote from the majority of citizens — for instance infringements of the liberty of minorities — would get a 'no' from the respected voice of the judiciary. 'When the American people are intoxicated by passion or carried away by the impetuosity of their ideas, they are checked and stopped by the almost invisible influence of their legal counsellors.'

The long fight to pass the federal anti-lynching law of 1934 and its limited success at stopping that barbaric practice are evidence of how law may be only partially effective in restraining the unjust impulses of majorities. The separation of the law from direct democratic influence is important in this respect. In Britain, this separation is maintained by the arcane and 'undemocratic' system by which judges are appointed. In the United States, where judges are mostly elected, the independence of the judiciary is more vulnerable. Many attempts have been made by politicians to alter the composition of the Supreme Court, starting with President Jefferson's attempt to have Justice Samuel Chase removed by impeachment in 1804. That case was won in Chase's favour; but in 1987 the political elimination of a Supreme Court judge was finally accomplished when a Democratic Senate rejected the nomination of the Republican Robert Bork. Political place-persons now pack the Supreme Court. Many of the greatest figures in American history have been lawyers with a high sense of what is right, demanding of the American people, both in public speeches and by legal process, a deference to principles of justice and respect for others. The politicization of law can only inhibit this supply of great individuals.

In terms of America's actions in the world, domestic law is of secondary importance. Every United States general is now accompanied by a lawyer while abroad to advise him what he may and may not do. The trouble is, a respect for law is all very well and good when there is a substantial body of law to respect; when there is very little effective law at all, as there is at present in the international arena, respect for it is scant good for anyone. That is the subject of the next chapter.

CHAPTER 8

International Law

One of the personae America has agreed to take on, reluctantly
it would have us believe, is that of the world's policeman. The
difference between America and a normal policeman is that
when a normal policeman comes knocking on your door, you
are reassured to know that he is subject to the restraints of the
law. When Policeman America knocks on your door he is liable
to trash the place, kill some of your family, and seize your
assets to repair at considerable profit to himself the damage he
has caused.

There is no comeback to this behaviour in international law
because there really is very little effective international law.
What is called 'international law' is mostly a series of instrumental rules for adjudicating between the interests of states
who subscribe to various treaties and conventions. Most of
these international treaties and conventions cover practicalities
and protocols of trade. If a state has not subscribed to an international convention which makes a particular activity — such
as the murder of foreign nationals — illegal, there is no international jurisdiction over such activity by that state.

So when the American president boasts that he has had foreign nationals murdered, as President Bush has done by impli-
cation several times since September 11th 2001, there is no
suggestion that he or anyone else might be prosecuted for their
murder, because America has not subscribed to any convention which would make such murders illegal. The war against
terror at present amounts to an informal war against enemies
whom America is free to define — public opinion allowing —

and against whom it may use lethal force as it chooses, so long as that lethal force takes place abroad.

A rule of law has four components, all of which must be regarded as authoritative by those who are to be ruled. First, there must be a recognized body of people who decide what the law should be. Second, there must be an apparatus for identifying possible breaches of the law. Third, there must be courts of law in which it can be determined whether the law has been broken in a particular case or not, and what the resulting sanction should be if it has. Fourth, there must be a method of enforcing the penalty decided upon by the court. All these elements must be generally recognized as authoritative and not in practice be obstructed.

That such a multi-tiered and complex authority should gain recognition and be effective across the globe might seem an impossibility. But there are still added complications.

First there is the question, are individuals or states to be the subjects of this rule of law? If individuals, then are they to be subject at the same time to two different systems of law, one national and one international? If, on the other hand, nations are to be the legal subjects, the same problems exist as do with corporate personae; for instance, how do you effectively penalize a country?

Next is the question, what are these laws designed to outlaw? Merely acts of aggression between states, just as domestic law concerns acts of injustice between individuals? Only crimes so gross as to constitute crimes against humanity? Or are they to impose one conception of the law across all of humanity — as the Belgians tried to do recently, to general ridicule?

It might be argued that at this stage we should opt for a basic minimum, and that is what the two attempts at international law currently in operation are trying to do.

The United Nations is the obvious base for an attempt at international law, and the International Court of Justice already exists as part of the United Nations. It has 'a dual role: to settle in accordance with international law the legal disputes submitted to it by states, and to give advisory opinions on legal questions referred to it by duly authorized international agencies and agencies.' These duly authorized bodies are all at present organs or agencies of the United Nations. The extent of its legal remit is summarized as follows:

Statute of the International Court of Justice, June 26, 1945:
ARTICLE 38

1. The Court, whose function is to decide in accordance with international law such disputes as are submitted to it, shall apply:

a. international conventions, whether general or particular, establishing rules expressly recognized by the contesting states;

b. international custom, as evidence of a general practice accepted as law;

c. the general principles of law recognized by civilized nations;

d. subject to the provisions of Article 59, judicial decisions and the teachings of the most highly qualified publicists of the various nations, as subsidiary means for the determination of rules of law.[1]

2. This provision shall not prejudice the power of the Court to decide a case *en aequo et bono*, if the parties agree thereto.

The International Criminal Court, meanwhile, is attempting to gather enough authority to prosecute individuals for war crimes and genocide. At present, this gathering of authority is being actively obstructed by the United States, which is refusing to sign the convention ratifying it. While pressure builds on the US to sign, it is entering into treaties with other states to reciprocally refuse to hand over each others' nationals to the jurisdiction of the court.

The stated objections of the United States are that many of the court's decisions to prosecute are politically motivated, and

---

[1] Article 59 states: The decision of the Court has no binding force except between the parties and in respect of that particular case.

that the court is not under supervision of the UN Security Council. It is widely assumed that the US is worried on several counts. Firstly, eminent American citizens have done things which might be viewed as criminal. Some are openly admitted, like Zbigniew Brszinski's boast that he used the CIA to provoke Russia's invasion of Afghanistan, like the saturation bombing of Cambodia under Nixon and Kissinger and like Bush's boasts that he has had people murdered. Secondly, everyone has it in for America because they are the most powerful nation on earth and this, in their role as the world's policeman, exposes them to excessive and biased scrutiny from the world community. Thirdly, since they are a country with a respect for law and its process, they would be more vulnerable than other countries should a decision be made to prosecute one of their citizens. To join in the process of developing international law would be to commit themselves to a process that the current administration neither wants nor needs.

All in all, the project for the impartial rule of international law seems fraught with difficulties. It is hard to imagine there being an effective rule of law across the globe in the near future, even should it limit itself to war crimes, genocide and aggression between states. The old complaint by Ma'arri's tired wife, 'People commit huge crimes, having learnt only petty acts earn hell fire,' seems set to run and run.

In particular, it seems impossible that the spread of 'weapons of mass destruction' could be contained by a simple and impartial rule of law. The US and other powers would hardly give up their own weapons of mass destruction while there is a possibility of other states sneakily manufacturing their own. The possibility of a world authority being authorized to maintain a monopoly of such weapons, and monitor the possibility of their development elsewhere, seems hardly likely unless that authority was constituted under the auspices of the United States, with the consent of all other nations via the United Nations. Proposals of this kind were made by both sides during the Cold War, though there was never enough trust to take them forward.

In the past, imperial powers imposed one law across their empires — their own. No doubt many corruptions and inequalities occurred, but at least there was rule of law of a sort. The avoidance of any formal empire-building by the Americans is partly due to their anti-imperial past, partly due to the inexpediency of actually running an empire — it being more profitable in the short term to seek commercial advantage and avoid sovereign responsibility — and partly due to changed conditions that make true empire-building impossible and/or unacceptable. This means that, for the foreseeable future, *pax Americana* is a misnomer. 'Savage small wars, often undeclared, have been essential to the growth and projection of American power', declares the blurb of one recent book extolling such conflicts. These wars can now be conducted with a one-sided savagery that knows no limits, nuclear weapons always being a possibility. Opposition can only come from the continual drip-drip attrition of 'terrorism'. Only an effective international law can stop this vicious circle.

Meanwhile, a situation develops where day by day it is more acceptable to boast of foreign murder. 'And they will know the meaning of American justice!' says President Bush, thrilling his supporters with the knowledge that enemies of America are being killed without trial or process of law. These killings are mostly carried out far from public knowledge or scrutiny; only when the event can hardly be hidden, or the victim is well-known, is the murder to be declared and boasted about. Some shame still attaches to acts of illegal depravity.

Reports appear in the newspapers, without stirring much notice, that America is shipping prisoners off to Jordan and Egypt for torture. One would have thought that the majority enthusiasm here might be, in de Tocquville's words, 'checked and stopped by the invisible influence of legal counsellors.' But it seems we are entering a time when both the spirit and letter of law are weak, just when we most need them to be strong.

War Without End, Amen

If you can get people to believe they are under attack, you can get them to do anything. attributed to Goebbels, Nazi propaganda minister

At some point we may be the only ones left. But that's okay with me. We are America.[1] George Bush Jnr., reported by Bob Woodward

War is one circumstance in which most people are prepared to give up some of their freedoms. Forgetting for a while internal strifes, a nation joins in a common purpose: to defeat the enemy. Afterwards, when peace returns, some of these freedoms may be returned, though not all: governments are a little sneaky and like to hang on to their hard-won powers.

The common purpose of war can be a subject for nostalgia after the war is over. Having got used to a feeling of community, solidarity and sacrifice, making something of life as a free agent seems a hard and lonely affair.

Warfare has changed over the centuries, advancing hand in hand with technology. It is often the motor impulse behind technological advance, as countries develop new technologies to stay ahead in the race to be better and better armed. Gunpowder was invented many centuries ago; it was then a long while before high explosives upped the ante; but in the last century the possibilities of mass destruction seem to have multiplied exponentially. Poison gas, used in the war of 1914–18 was

---

[1] The president was apparently referring to America's coalition against Iraq, not survival on Earth.

the first dramatic newcomer; after that came, in quick succession, rockets and missiles, biological weapons, the nuclear bomb, and now the host of possibilities outlined below.

The Project for a New American Century is a document widely available on the Internet. It was written by members of the current US administration before they came to power. Mostly an exposition on how America should build on its world preeminence, it contains the following analysis of the possibilities of modern warfare opened up by science. The paragraph below describes a scenario for world political control which makes the alternative to some kind of global legal authority seem horrible beyond contemplation. The idea of this technology being used by any power, let alone several powers in opposition, to control the lives of citizens is a horror beyond science fiction. If this is to become science fact, it might seem to our descendants better off not to have been born. The final sentence seems to imply that a nation — or world? — free of undesirable races ('specific genotypes') might be a 'political' objective of the project.

Real life is not supposed to imitate sick jokes, but there was a joke circulating at the time of the build-up to the war with Iraq which went like this. George Bush and Saddam meet up to discuss things. Saddam is telling Mr Bush how much he enjoys Star Trek. 'But there's one thing that puzzles me', says Saddam. 'You have a black person, a woman, even a Scotsman on board! But why no Muslim?' 'That's because it's about the future, Saddam', the president replies.

> Although it may take several decades for the process of transformation to unfold, in time, the art of warfare on air, land, and sea will be vastly different than it is today, and 'combat' likely will take place in new dimensions: in space, 'cyber-space,' and perhaps the world of microbes. Air warfare may no longer be fought by pilots manning tactical fighter aircraft sweeping the skies of opposing fighters, but a regime dominated by long-range, stealthy unmanned craft. On land, the clash of massive, combined-arms armored forces may be replaced by the dashes of much lighter, stealthier and information-intensive forces, augmented by fleets of robots, some small enough to fit in soldiers' pockets. Control of the sea could be largely determined not by fleets of surface combatants and aircraft carriers, but from land- and space-based sys-

tems, forcing navies to maneuver and fight underwater. Space itself will become a theater of war, as nations gain access to space capabilities and come to rely on them; further, the distinction between military and commercial space systems — combatants and noncombatants — will become blurred. Information systems will become an important focus of attack, particularly for U.S. enemies seeking to short-circuit sophisticated American forces. And advanced forms of biological warfare that can 'target' specific genotypes may transform biological warfare from the realm of terror to a politically useful tool.

The Project for a New American Century

Bibliography

Acton, John, *Essays in the History of Liberty*, Liberty Fund (1985).

Bicheno, Hugh, and Holmes, Richard, *Rebels and Redcoats: The American Revolutionary War*, Harper Collins (2003).

Blum, William, *Rogue State: A Guide to the World's Only Superpower*, Common Courage Press (2000).

Burckhardt, Jacob, *On History and Historians*, Liberty Fund (1999).

Burckhardt, Jacob, *Reflections on History*, Liberty Fund (1979).

Carey, John, *The Intellectuals and the Masses: Pride and Prejudice Among the Literary Intelligentsia, 1880-1939*, Academy Chicago (2002).

Cather, Willa, *One of Ours*, Virago (1987).

Ceaser, James, *Reconstructing America: The Symbol of America in Modern Thought*, Yale University Press (2000).

Darlington, C.D., *The Evolution of Man and Society*, Allen and Unwin (1969).

Darlington, C.D., *The Little Universe of Man*, Allen and Unwin (1978).

de Tocqueville, Alexis, *Democracy in America*, Everyman (1994).

Jeffreys-Jones, R., *The CIA and American Democracy*, Yale University Press (1989).

Joly, Eva, *Est-ce dans ce monde-là que nous voulons vivre?*, Editions des Arènes (2003).

Mandelstam, Nadezhda, *Hope Against Hope*, Modern Library (1999).

Mandelstam, Nadezhda, *Hope Abandoned*, Macmillan (1981).

Mosley, Ivo (ed.), Dumbing Down: Politics, Culture and the Mass Media, Imprint Academic (2000).

Oakeshott, Michael, 'A Place of Learning', in *The Voice of Liberal Learning*, Yale University Press (1989).

Oakeshott, Michael, 'Leviathan, *A Myth*' in *Hobbes on Civil Association*, Yale University Press (1989).

Oakeshott, Michael, 'The Rule of Law' in *On History and Other Essays*, Liberty Fund (1999).

Polanyi, Michael, *The Logic of Liberty: Reflections and Rejoinders*, Liberty Fund (1998).

Potok, Chaim, *Wanderings: Chaim Potok's History of the Jews*, Fawcett Books (1990).

Rieff, Philip, *The Feeling Intellect: Selected Writings*, University of Chicago Press (1990).

Russell, Conrad, *The Crisis of Parliaments*, Oxford University Press (1971).

Shiva, Vandana, *Protect or Plunder?: Understanding Intellectual Property Rights*, Zed Books (2001).

Sutherland, Keith (ed.), *The Rape of the Constitution*, Imprint Academic (2000).

von Mises, Ludwig, *Socialism: An Economic and Sociological Analysis*, Jonathan Cape (1951).

Webb, Sidney, in G.B. Shaw (ed.), *Fabian Essays in Socialism*, Peter Smith Publishing (1981).

West, E.G., *Education and the State: A Study in Political Economy*, Liberty Fund (1994).

West, M.L, *Greek Lyric Poetry*, Clarendon Press (1993).

Wilson, William Julius, *When Work Disappears*, Vintage Books (1997).

Zane, John M., *The Story of Law*, Liberty Fund (1998).

Zepezauer, Mark, *Boomerang! How Our Covert Wars Have Created Enemies Across the Middle East and Brought Terror to America*, Common Courage Press (2002).

essays in political and cultural criticism

Contemporary public debate has been impoverished by two competing trends. On the one hand the increasing commercialisation of the visual media has meant that in-depth commentary has given way to the ten-second soundbite. On the other hand the explosion of scholarly knowledge has led to such a degree of specialisation that academic discourse has ceased to be comprehensible. As a result writing on politics and culture tends to be either superficial or baffling.

This was not always so—especially in the field of politics. The high point of the English political pamphlet was the seventeenth century, when a number of small printer-publishers responded to the political ferment of the age with an outpouring of widely-accessible pamphlets and tracts. Indeed Imprint Academic operates a reprint service under the banner of 'The Rota', offering facsimile editions of works such as *The World's Mistake in Oliver Cromwell.*

In recent years the tradition of the political pamphlet has declined—with most publishers rejecting anything under 100,000 words as uneconomic. The result is that many a good idea has ended up drowning in a sea of verbosity. However the introduction of the digital press makes it possible to re-create a more exciting age of publishing. *Societas* authors are all experts in their own field, either scholarly or professional, but the essays are aimed at a general audience. Each book should take no more than an evening to read.

The books are available through the retail trade at the price of £8.95/$17.90 each, or on bi-monthly subscription for only £5.00/$10.50.Full details and forthcoming title information from Imprint Academic:

www.imprint-academic.com/societas

IMPRINT ACADEMIC, PO Box 200, Exeter, EX5 5YX, UK
Tel: (0)1392 841600   Fax: (0)1392 841478   Email: sandra@imprint.co.uk

Democracy, Fascism and the New World Order
Ivo Mosley

Growing up as the grandson of the 1930s blackshirt leader, made Ivo Mosley consider fascism with a deep interest. Whereas conventional wisdom sets up democracy and fascism as opposites, to ancient political theorists democracy had an innate tendency to lead to extreme populist government, and provided demagogues with the opportunity to seize power. This book argues that totalitarian regimes can be the outcome of unfettered mass democracy.

SOCIETAS   96 pp., £8.95/$14.95, 0907845 649

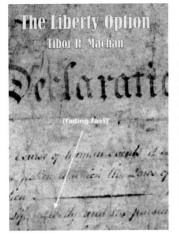

The Liberty Option
Tibor R. Machan

The Liberty Option advances the idea that for compelling moral and practical reasons it is the society organised on classical liberal principles that serves justice best, leads to prosperity and encourages the greatest measure of individual virtue. The book contrasts the Lockean ideal with the various statist alternatives, defends it against its communitarian critics and lays out some of its more significant policy implications. Machan is a research fellow at Stanford University's Hoover Institution. He has written extensively on classical liberal theory, including *Classical Individualism* (Routledge, 1998).

SOCIETAS   104 pp., £8.95/$14.95, 0907845 630

new, updated edition

The Last Prime Minister
Graham Allen MP

Echoing Gandhi's comment on Western civilization, Graham Allen thinks the British constitution would be a very good idea. In *The Last Prime Minister* he showed the British people how they had acquired an executive presidency by stealth. This timely new edition takes in new issues, including Parliament's constitutional impotence over Iraq.

'Sharp, well-informed and truly alarming.' **Peter Hennessy**
'Iconoclastic, stimulating and well-argued, it's publication could hardly be more timely.' **Vernon Bogdanor, THES**

SOCIETAS   96 pp. £8.95/$14.95 0907845 41X

sample chapters, reviews and TOCs: www.imprint-academic.com/societas

SOCIETAS